Blood Prairie

Perilous Adventures on the Oklahoma Frontier

Ron J. Jackson, Jr.

EAKIN PRESS Fort Worth, Texas
www.EakinPress.com

Copyright © 2007
By Ron J. Jackson, Jr.
Published By Eakin Press
An Imprint of Wild Horse Media Group
P.O. Box 331779
Fort Worth, Texas 76163
1-817-344-7036
www.EakinPress.com
ALL RIGHTS RESERVED
1 2 3 4 5 6 7 8 9
Paperback ISBN 978-1-68179-326-9
Hardback ISBN 978-1-68179-328-3
eBook ISBN 978-1-68179-327-6

ALL RIGHTS RESERVED. No part of this book may be reproduced in any form without written permission from the publisher, except for brief passages included in a review appearing in a newspaper or magazine.

"I fear that the conquest of savagery in the Southwest was due more often to love of adventure than to any wish that cities should arise in the desert, or that highways of civilization should take place of the Indian and the buffalo. In fact, many of us believed and hoped that the wilderness would remain forever. Life was to our liking. Its freedom, its dangers, its tax upon our strength and courage, gave zest to living …"

Frontier Scout Billy Dixon,
Cimarron County, Oklahoma

*To Jeannia,
My Frontier Scout …*

Contents

Summer Of Sorrow / 3
From The Darkness / 19
Revenge On The Long Knives / 37
Merciless Frontier / 57
Buffalo Wallow Fight / 71

Oklahoma History Timeline / 95
Endnotes / 105

Introduction

My parents raised me to dream. So I did.

Looking back now at my childhood in California, dreaming seemed to come naturally, as if bestowed upon me by God or the sunshine that often draped the golden hills framing my hometown of Vacaville. Dreaming, I concluded early in life, was the inalienable right of every Californian.

Dare to dream. Dare to live.

This has been my motto through good times and bad. And as months have toppled into years, I've grown to believe my dreams spring from the roots of my California pride and upbringing. Everywhere I turned as a child, I was exposed to the spirit of pioneers who dared to chase their dreams.

I've climbed narrow passes in the Sierra Nevada Mountains where gold prospectors risked their lives in search of their fortunes. Most returned empty handed, save for the wealth they had accumulated in adventure.

I've visited the haunts of old San Francisco where tens of thousands flocked during the wild days of '49, en route for the gold fields along the Sacramento River and beyond. The Gold Rush dashed countless dreams, prompting disenchanted prospectors to sail away and never look back. Other folks, through either hard work or good fortune, remained behind to carve out a future and a new city.

They would build something special.

San Francisco is now a world-renown port city, the heartbeat of which was borne from industrious first- and second-generation immigrants from Ireland, England, Italy, Germany, Poland, and China.

I've also walked in the footsteps of Walt Disney, a dreamer who turned a forgotten orchard into a Magic Kingdom.

"You can be anything you want to be," my father used to tell me in quiet moments. "Just remember, you don't have to be the best. You can be one of the best."

So in 1996, I bid farewell to my native California in search of my own dreams in the wide-open spaces of western Oklahoma. My wife and I sought a humble piece of prairie, a place where we could spread our elbows and raise our children in a wholesome environment.

We stuffed everything we owned in a moving van, emptied our bank accounts, and journeyed to Oklahoma without any jobs. We did so because we dared to dream. Within two months, I found steady employment at *The Oklahoman* newspaper in Oklahoma City, where I proudly continue to work as a reporter.

During my free time, I pursue my other great passion as an historical author.

Long ago, perhaps as a child clad in a Davy Crockett

coonskin cap, I became smitten by history. One of my earliest memories was watching John Wayne in the role of Crockett in his movie epic, *The Alamo*. In my mind, I too made my last stand from the warmth of my living room, fighting to the death with Wayne and every other Alamo defender in the name of independence.

Even then, I remember being moved by men who would unselfishly trade their lives for freedom in the face of overwhelming odds. The Texas story continues to stir my blood to this day, and I recently finished a manuscript for my second Alamo-related book – an historical biography of a mulatto slave who survived the 1836 siege and battle.

My frequent ventures into Texas for research and pleasure have allowed me to forge life-long friendships. Along the way, I discovered something similar to my California pride – Texas pride. Texans are fiercely proud of their history, and rightfully so. After all, they do have the Alamo.

Texans, I have come to understand, also dare to dream – Texas-sized dreams, naturally. But my good friends to the south do have one minor failing when it comes to history. They believe history begins at the Rio Grande and ends at the Red River.

Oklahomans, by contrast, are comparatively quiet when it comes to their history. Oklahoma natives have psychoanalyzed their collective silence in that respect for me by suggesting it's borne from the stigma of the Great Depression and Dust Bowl, when starving Okies fled to California for survival. They suggest that's why Oklahomans today rally in virtual unison around the winning tradition of the University of Oklahoma Sooners football program. The Sooners have delivered seven national championships to the good folks of Oklahoma, and in doing so have provided a great source of pride throughout their glorious history.

Football is therefore king in Oklahoma.

Yet I would argue Oklahomans – and Americans everywhere, for that matter – have generally sold Oklahoma history far too short. Oklahoma cradles some of the most unique and storied episodes in American history – sagas as captivating as any other state in the Union.

Oklahoma is home to those who survived the Trail of Tears, drove cattle along the Chisholm Trail, fought in the Plains Indian Wars, and participated in the great land runs of 1889, 1892, and 1893.

What other state can boast the epic of a nationally publicized run for land? None. Pioneers from all walks of life found equal footing on the Oklahoma plains in 1889. All they had to do was dare to dream, and they too could stake a claim on a patch of land to call their own. They rode trains, horses, wagons, schooners, and even bicycles in search of a better tomorrow.

Along the way they carved crude dugout dwellings out of the red soil, or erected shacks or log cabins, and busily went to work building a future for themselves and their families. They began with little more than the land and their dreams.

In the end, like the legendary pioneers of San Francisco, they too built something special.

Oklahoma's saga is collectively a triumphant one. Consider one of Oklahoma's darkest chapters, the forced removal of thousands of Indians along the Trail of Tears in the 1830s. Today, descendants of those survivors are proud leaders and working class heroes in their respective nations and communities. They honor their ancestors by living productive lives, raising families, and never forgetting to pass down the tribal stories to the next generation.

I hope to accomplish something similar with this humble, little manuscript as my adopted home state celebrates its centennial. *Blood Prairie* pays tribute to the sacrifices of those who lived on Oklahoma's enchanting, yet often violent, prairie. Within these pages, one will quickly realize Oklahoma is sacred ground.

"Summer of Sorrow" and "Revenge On The Long Knives" – two articles that originally appeared in *True West Magazine* – are gripping sagas of a time when blood flowed freely on the Oklahoma frontier as cultures clashed. Sometimes, those clashes went beyond the stereotypical confrontation of an Indian nation and the white man's world. Sometimes, Indians clashed with Indians.

This book also offers a Civil War battle through the eyes of an Indian Territory slave, the bloody history of a Mexican captive, and a slightly new twist on the Buffalo

Wallow Fight when a handful of soldiers made a desperate last stand against hundreds of warring Indians. The Buffalo Wallow Fight is a fine example of the promotional juggernaut known as Texas. True, the Buffalo Wallow Fight occurred in the Texas Panhandle, but nearly every participant – white and red – hailed from Oklahoma. Two heroes of the Buffalo Wallow engagement – scouts Amos Chapman and Billy Dixon – even lived their final days in Oklahoma, as did many of their Indian foes. Somehow, this aspect of the story has been either overlooked or underplayed.

Not this time.

Oklahoma belongs front and center in the annals of western American history. Oklahomans, meanwhile, should take great pride in their heritage. For even in the darkest of episodes they will find the light of victory. Settlers fought to conquer the frontier. Indians refused to be conquered. Slaves died to be free. Ultimately, Oklahomans should find inspiration in knowing they live in a land where these pioneers dared to chase their dreams.

I have.

— Ron J. Jackson, Jr.

Summer of Sorrow

Hunting Horse photo courtesy of Western History Collection, University of Oklahoma

The Kiowa elder Hunting Horse maneuvered gingerly over a rugged terrain chalked with granite rocks and boulders until he could see the vibrant, green canyon below. He was flanked by relatives who guided his every step and waited patiently for the venerable elder to speak.

Nearby, on this warm afternoon in the late 1940s, stood a teenage Jack Haley whose family owned the ridge from which the small group stood. He too waited intently.

Behind them towered the majestic, western ridge of the Wichita Mountains—a granite monument of sorts for pioneers who ventured across Oklahoma's western plains. For Hunting Horse and his Kiowa brethren, the Wichita Mountains also held a special meaning.

The ground was sacred to the Kiowa, christened over 100 years earlier with the blood of their ancestors.

Keenly, the frail Hunting Horse panned the canyon below with eyes that had seen over 100 years of life and with a heart heavy from the knowledge he carried within. Hunting Horse had visited the canyon many times before with his mother, and on this day, he would eloquently retell her story.[1] It was a saga of survival and sorrow from the summer of 1833—a time recorded on Kiowa calendars as *Imk odalta-de Pai*: "Summer that they cut off their heads."[2]

Finally, above the howl of the wind, the old man's voice could be heard.

Panic spread throughout the Kiowa village one day in the summer of 1833. Word arrived of an encounter by warriors with an Osage war party on the plains near present-day Caddo County, Oklahoma. A violent struggle ensued. One Osage was wounded. One Kiowa laid dead.

Others reported seeing an Osage arrow protruding from the carcass of a buffalo.

Neither account bode well for the Kiowa tribe, which had developed a terror of the Osage. Rooted in the fears of the Kiowa was the knowledge their northern enemy possessed a far deadlier weapon than any they owned—the flintlock rifle. Osage warriors had acquired rifles, as well as other goods such as long knives, from eastern traders and had become the scourge of southern tribes who crossed their path.

At the time of the discovery the Kiowa village laid sprawled where the Rainy Mountain Creek flowed into the rushing waters of the Washita River. Alarmed by the news, the tranquil encampment soon became distraught with the anticipation of an Osage attack. A large party of Kiowa warriors who had planned to go north on a raiding expedition against the Utes postponed their departure. Men, women and children dug into the dirt on the Washita River's southern bank and threw up crude, earthen works for defense.[3]

There they waited. And waited.

Scouts scoured the countryside for signs of an Osage war party. Each returned to camp with nothing new to report. Several days passed without incident as the Osage had seemingly vanished.

Calmed by the days of silence, the Kiowa warriors eventually left camp for their raiding party against the Utes. Mostly old men, women and children were left behind to guard the village. Those who remained then decided to disperse into several smaller bands—one going southeast to Eagle Heart Springs, near the headwaters of Cache Creek.

This band, led by an elderly chief named *A'date* (Island Man), soon moved westward through a pass in the Wichita Mountains and into a plush, green canyon speckled with wildflowers and cedar trees. Sloping gently below a ridge at one end of the canyon was a spacious meadow, flanked by a modest rocky hill to the south and the banks of Otter Creek to the north. A vast, open prairie laid to the west.

Here, nestled in the shadow of the Wichita Mountains, *A'date*'s followers again set up camp and waited for the return of their raiding party.

Skinned tepees and campfires soon dotted the

meadow, a place of enchantment for the Kiowa people. A large spring flowed from a granite ledge nearby, and mammoth elm and cottonwood trees shaded the curved creek banks. Wild blackberries and plum thickets were scattered throughout the area, which was also teaming with an abundance of deer, rabbits, turkeys and other wildlife.[4]

To the east, corralled by the natural contour of the mountain range, a herd of an estimated 400 Kiowa horses grazed amid the tall, prairie grass in the canyon above the ridge. The tribe had hoped to breed its horses with the hardier stock of wild stallions that roamed the mountains.[5]

Peace had again prevailed among the Kiowa. Soon, so would terror.

A group of frightened Kiowa girls returned to camp one evening with word they had seen a strange warrior at a nearby pond. Elders brushed off the story as the pranks of a few of the camp's ornery boys.[6]

Prior to sunrise the next day, one Kiowa boy arose early to check his ponies grazing in the canyon. As he reached the crest of the ridge he noticed the shaven head of an Osage warrior bobbing behind some boulders on the open canyon floor.

Instantly, the boy ran back to the camp to alert the sleeping villagers.[7]

Sematma (Apache Woman), wife of chief *A'date*, was already awake. She was preparing to scrape a hide. Hearing the boy's cry, *Sematma* rushed into her tepee to

Stumbling Bear photo courtesy of Western History Collection, University of Oklahoma

Kiowa Encampment courtesy of Western History Collection, University of Oklahoma

awake her husband, who emerged yelling, *"Tso' batso! Tso' batso!"*—"To the rocks! To the rocks!"

His plea was too late.

Osage warriors swarmed the stunned village from all directions, charging on foot from behind trees, rocks and thick brush. They pounced on the panic-stricken women and children still drowsy from sleep and killed at will.

One old warrior named *An zah te* was so terrified he ran away without his war shield, an inexcusable display of cowardice for a Kiowa warrior.[8]

An-so te, keeper of the Kiowa's *Taime* medicine, surrendered the sacred idols to the Osage in his desperate flight to safety. His wife wasn't so fortunate. She was killed while trying to unfasten the *Taime* from a tepee pole.[9]

Sematma was also captured, but later lived to tell of her escape. *A'date* escaped with a slight wound.[10]

Those who scrambled to the small mountain were chased down and quickly butchered. Children were swung by the ankles and bashed against the rocks. Others were pulled from the rattlesnake-infested crevices of the craggy mountain before being slaughtered. Several Kiowa women were remembered for defending their children to the death.[11]

Heroic deeds that day became legendary among the Kiowa.

One woman, carrying an infant girl on her back, fled while dragging an older girl in tow. When a pursuing

Osage grabbed the older girl and drew a knife to her throat, the woman viciously beat off the attacker. All three survived as the older girl escaped with a slight gash.

A boy named *Aya* (Sitting On A Tree) was saved in a similar way by his father.[12] *Aya*'s father snatched his cradle in flight, stopping several times to shoot arrows at his pursuers. He shot with the buckskin thongs of his son's cradle clenched in his teeth.[13]

A Pawnee warrior living in the camp fought off Osage attackers long enough to give a group of women time to make their escape.

Some even saw one Kiowa boy place himself between the onrushing Osage and the fleeing women and children. The boy shot arrow after arrow.

One Kiowa woman told her daughter to run while she turned and met the enemy with a tomahawk. She too miraculously escaped.[14]

Survivors too young to remember the attack would be told in the years to come how fate spared them on that blackest of Kiowa days. Among those lucky ones would be a three-year-old boy named *Set-Imkia* (Stumbling Bear), who was carried to safety and went on to become a prestigious Kiowa statesmen. *Set-Imkia* was the Kiowa's principal chief at the time of his death in 1866.[15]

One old Kiowa man, whose name history has lost, escaped on foot to the north across Otter Creek. He continued his frantic flight to the west for many miles in hopes of finding one of the other Kiowa camps, but stumbled instead upon a Cheyenne village. The Cheyenne people gathered around as the old man gave his account of the hellish attack.

Cheyenne warriors immediately sprang upon their horses, wasting no time to saddle them, and raced toward the bloody scene of the Kiowa village. Osage warriors could be seen leaving the village as they arrived, and the Cheyennes rode all out in pursuit.

The chase ended when the Cheyenne horses gave out.[16]

Shortly thereafter the returning Kiowa raiders discovered what the Cheyenne warriors had a few days earlier in the meadow along Otter Creek. Mangled and disfigured bodies of fellow tribal members laid strewn about the looted and torched village.

Osage warriors left one more ghastly reminder of their visit. Brass buckets obtained by the Kiowa from Pawnee traders were mockingly placed in a row amid the destroyed village and filled with the severed heads of their victims.[17]

Individual accounts of gallantry and sorrow began to surface as the mourning survivors reunited with the Kiowa warriors one by one. Stories of narrow escapes and savagery were told. Other details were related. Gone were two children—a brother and a sister—who had been taken captive. Gone was the Kiowa's magnificent horse herd. And gone was the tribe's sacred *Taime*, torn from the hands of the *Taime* keeper's dying wife.

Without the *Taime*, the Kiowa people did not have

the spiritual medicine to hold their annual Sun Dance. So there was no Sun Dance in the summer of 1833. Only sorrow.

An estimated 150 of the Kiowa's 2,000 people died in the massacre, most of whom were women and children.[18] Five Kiowa men were also counted among the dead—no Osage.[19]

A mass grave was created from a deep impression in the ground near Otter Creek, where the dead were ceremoniously laid and covered with rocks and dirt. Among the victims of the massacre was one Kiowa chief who had participated in a successful raid against American traders the previous winter. He was buried along with his share of the spoils from that raid—a batch of silver dollars.[20]

A little girl said goodbye to her best friend by placing a lock of her hair next to his remains. The boy ran into the arms of the girl at the front of her teepee. Blood covered his body from an arrow wound. The boy soon died in the girl's arms, leaving her drenched in her friend's blood.

Shortly afterward, the girl's mother was also killed by her side as the screams echoed around her teepee. Terrified, the girl pulled the lifeless bodies of her friend and mother over her and played dead until the screams disappeared.

The girl then made a successful break for safety only to carry the mental scars of a survivor.[21]

Chief *A'date* became another casualty of the massacre in the weeks to follow when he was removed in disgrace by a tribal council for his inability to protect his followers. In his place arose the leadership of a young warrior named *Dohasen*.

Contact by the Kiowa for the first time with United States soldiers also came in the wake of the massacre. U.S. Dragoons stationed at Fort Gibson purchased the two Kiowa children taken captive from the Osage, and then arranged for their return the following summer. A group of Osage warriors were persuaded to accompany the dragoons as a goodwill gesture.

George Catlin, the legendary 19th-century western artist, painted the two children a few days before their scheduled departure from Fort Gibson. The boy, *Tunk-aht-oh-ye* (The Thunderer), died a day after posing for Catlin's painting when he was struck in the abdomen and knocked against a fence by a ram at a fur trader's house. Catlin later wrote, "He was a beautiful boy of nine or ten years of age ..."

Wun-pan-to-me (The White Weasel), the boy's sister, thus made the long journey home to her people in mourning.[22]

Dohasen later successfully negotiated with the Osage for the return of the *Taime*, ending the two-year absence of the Sun Dance. Peace with the Osage had been made, but the atrocities at Otter Creek would never be forgotten.[23]

Of this future generations of Kiowa people would make certain.

The elder ranchman and retired archivist Jack Haley gingerly walked over a rugged terrain chalked with granite rocks and boulders until he could see the vibrant, green canyon below. He leaned on a long, dulled cedar cane, and recalled how he had journeyed to this very location some 45 years earlier with the legendary Kiowa scout Hunting Horse.

Nearby, on this warm afternoon in 1999, stood a visitor who waited intently to hear what Hunting Horse had once told Haley about the canyon's role in the most tragic episode in Kiowa history. Over the years countless tribal elders like Hunting Horse had journeyed to Haley's property to pay their respects to those who died there.

On still, quiet evenings Haley has heard the distant chants of Kiowa medicine men roll down from the mountain behind his home. He has even heard the tales of the haunting spirits who are believed to still wander the area at night.

Haley stirred his memory by panning the canyon below.

Finally, above the howl of the wind, the old man's voice could be heard.

Photo of rancher Jack Haley by Rita Giblet

From the Darkness

George W. Stidham, owner of Jim Tomm and his family, photo courtesy of Oklahoma Historical Society.

Little Jim Tomm's eyes darted about the darkened and crowded plantation cellar as the candlelight flickered off the dirt walls. Four-year-old Tomm huddled in the cellar with his mother, twin sisters, and a number of fellow slaves who belonged to George W. Stidham, a native Alabaman of Scotch-Irish and Creek Indian parentage.[1]

Stidham, a Creek judge, owned a plantation south of Fern Mountain, about a mile west of the Creek Agency near the present town of Rentiesville, Oklahoma.

None of the slaves had seen their master since the news of the Union Army's approach first began to circulate in the region. Stidham enlisted with the Second Regiment of the Creek Mounted Volunteers at the outbreak of the Civil War, but in the summer of 1863, he found refuge with his family and 30 of his most prized slaves south of the Red River. Tomm's father—a talented blacksmith—was among the bondsmen whom Stidham secreted away to Texarkana, Texas, where he purchased large tracts of land.

Stidham's remaining slaves, meanwhile, were left to fend for themselves at his Indian Territory plantation.

Despite his age, Tomm clearly comprehended the

drama that unfolded that summer night in the refuge beneath a hand-hewn log cabin—stark, heart-pounding images that would shadow him into old age. Years later Tomm would remember how "that night the cellar was full of folks under that house and scared to death."[2]

At daybreak, on July 17, 1863, Tomm peered out of his family's hiding place. He noticed the warmth of daylight, and saw the sun's rays shining through the cracks in the cabin walls.

But a storm brewed.

First, came the rain, which pelted the cabin's shake-shingle roof. Then came the roar of thunder and cannon fire—undistinguishable sounds from their underground hideout. The uncertainty of the moment rendered the slaves paralyzed by fear.

Would this be the day they met death?

Women—strong women—trembled. Elders worried. Children cried.

This is how the Civil War entered Jim Tomm's life . . .

The slave cabins might be one of the first things a visitor noticed on the Stidham plantation. Unlike slave quarters in Mississippi or Louisiana, Stidham's slave quarters were bunched together.

Stidham ordered them built in that manner when he first settled in the Creek Nation to guard against raids by "wild Indians" who still roamed the territory.

But the Plains Indians such as the Kiowa, Cheyenne, and Comanche followed the buffalo, and by the time Jim was born in 1859, the largest herds had been pushed westward.[3]

Still, the Creek Nation flourished with wild game. Fish could also be found teaming in every river, creek, and stream, and the birds flew in flocks so great they would sometimes blot out the sun.

The countryside additionally offered an abundance of wild fruits, such as a variety of berries. Nuts were also gathered in the fall and stored for the winter.

Tomm remembered the rare treat of buffalo meat. Osage Indians would sometimes travel from the north to sell buffalo to Stidham for his slaves, who because of its scarcity would cut the meat into small cubes. The cubes were then slid onto a string and hung in the sun to dry.

"All in all, the slaves lived good," Tomm recalled decades later. "They did not worry much. All they had to do was work and sleep and old Master took good care of them."[4]

They, in turn, took care of one another.

Life on the plantation was fairly peaceful for the slaves, who labored in a seasonal rhythm that gave order and a sense of serenity to their daily existence. They took pride in their work, and found unity in their shared quest for survival.

Shoes, for instance, were all made on the plantation by hand.

"A cow hide was tanned with bark," Tomm remembered. "The hair from the hide was removed with wood ashes. The soles were put on with wooden pegs, whittled out by the slaves. The uppers were sewed by hand, using waxed thread, hog bristles for needles and holes made with an awl. The thread was made on the spinning wheel and the bee-wax came from robbing wild bees."[5]

The ingenuity marveled a young Tomm.

"Soap was made by storing ashes in a hopper and pouring water on them and letting it drain slowly through the ashes and this would make a lye water," Tomm said. "The grease was fats from wild hogs and other animals. Lye water and grease boiled down made soap."[6]

Tom, Jim's father, held a special place of prominence on the Stidham plantation as blacksmith. All ox yokes, wagon riggings, and farming tools were made by Tom, who hammered them into shape at his blacksmith shop. Iron was obtained from nearby Fort Gibson.

Jim admired his father, and in the aftermath of the Civil War, adopted his first name as his surname. Hence, the name Jim Tomm. His parents—Flora and Tom—instead took the Stidham name after emancipation.

By then, Tom and Flora Stidham's life journey had already brought them far. Jim Tomm learned that his parents' life began in the deep south, where they labored on rice plantations in Louisiana and also lived peacefully among the Seminoles in Alabama and Mississippi on cotton plantations.

George Stidham purchased Flora in New Orleans. Flora had already given birth to four children by then. She would birth four more children after being relocated to the Indian Territory—Jim being the youngest.

Jim's family grew close in the Creek Nation, and it was that closeness that would later carry them through the numerous trials of bondage. Yet no crisis would prove greater for Jim's family and the slaves of Indian Territory than the Civil War.

The War Between the States—"the white man's war"—would rip Indian Territory apart, just as it did for people across the American north and south. People were divided over issues that were, at times, complex.

Indian Territory may have been as complex as any place within the United States in the Spring of 1861. The territory constituted a large reserve where various tribes were assigned lands, and when necessary, moved there by force in brutal marches that would become known as the Trail of Tears.

The most prominent among these tribes were the Five Civilized Tribes—the Cherokees, Chickasaws, Choctaws, Creeks, and Seminoles. Each tribe brought their traditional ways, as well as constitutionally recognized governments with schools, churches, and businesses.

They also brought slavery.

Slave populations varied from one tribal nation to

the next. Prior to removal in November 1811, the *Christian Observer* in London, for instance, reported 12,395 Cherokee Indians living in the southeastern region of the United States along with 583 black slaves. As cotton prices climbed, so too, did the slave population within the tribe.[7]

Cherokee slave owners held 1,592 black men, women, and children in bondage in 1835. By 1860, that number had risen to 2,511 slaves.[8]

Still, no tribe monopolized the business of human chattel in Indian Territory. Slaves also toiled for Chickasaw, Choctaw, Creek, and Seminole elites. Bitter divisions would eventually arise from these slave empires at the outbreak of the war.

More than 1,000 Creeks debated the issue of allegiance in July 1861 while encamped on the west bank of Baptizing Creek, some two miles west of present-day Eufaula. Emotions ran high as they decided whether to accept an offer to align with the Confederacy, or remain loyal to the Union.[9]

Stidham steadfastly pledged his allegiance to the Confederacy.

Others, like Chief Opothleyahola, argued against the abandonment of the old treaty with the federal government, which recognized the sovereignty of the Creek Nation. Unable to sway those assembled, Opothleyahola finally withdrew his support and led his followers into the northern frontier.

Opothleyahola and Ouktahanaserharjo (or Sands)

turned to President Abraham Lincoln for help the next month, asking the "Great Father" to remember his commitment to his Creek children. The letter, dated February 15, 1861, read in part:

> You said that in our new homes we should be defended from all interference from any people and that no white people in the whole world should ever molest us unless they came from the sky but the land should be ours as long as grass grew and waters run, and should we be injured by anybody you would come with your soldiers & punish them, but now the wolf has come, men who are strangers tread our soil, our children are frightened & the mothers cannot sleep for fear.[10]

Lincoln never responded.

By then, the division was already deep. Opposing Creeks at the North Fork Town council in July had signed a treaty to pledge allegiance to the Confederate States—one of the opening salvos to splinter tribes and families throughout the territory.

Slaveholders such as Stidham responded by carrying their most valuable slaves deeper into the south for protection, often leaving behind the weaker wives, children, or elders. Families—black, red, and white—were soon scattered to the wind.[11]

Emboldened slaves, sensing an opportunity to be free, seized their destiny by slipping off to the north during the days and months of upheaval.[12]

Opothleyahola's following grew overnight. By

September 1861, more than 7,000 supporters rallied around the venerable chief they affectionately called "Old Gouge," including mostly disenfranchised Creek and Seminole Indians. A number of runaway slaves also joined the mass exodus.[13]

Phoebe Banks, an infant slave at the time, later heard stories about the flight north from her father, William McIntosh, and uncle, Jacob Perryman. The two slaves led the other runaway slaves and their families, including Jim Tomm's older brother.[14]

"All our family join up with him (Opothleyahola), and there was lots of Creek Indians and slaves in the outfit when they made the break for the north," Banks recalled. "The runaways was riding ponies stolen from their masters."[15]

Violence shadowed them on their journey.

Banks heard riveting stories of the exodus many times growing up, noting how when they arrived in the hills "farther north in the country that belonged to the Cherokee Indians, they make camp on a big creek and there the Rebel Indian soldiers catch up, but they was fought back."[16]

By daybreak, the exodus resumed in great haste. The smallest children were strapped to the backs of horses, and iron kettles and other camp supplies were hurriedly slung over pack animals as they climbed further into the mountains.

Only the Rebel soldiers would return.

"The Creek Indians and the slaves with them try to

fight off them soldiers like they did before, but they get scattered around and separated so's they lose the battle," Banks said. "Lost their horses and wagons, and the soldiers killed lots of the Creeks and Negroes, and some of the slaves was captured and took back to their masters."[17]

The dead lay scattered throughout the hills. Wounded slaves continued to ride their horses with blood dripping down their saddles, some of whom fell off their mounts several miles from the battlefield.

Survivors rode past the wounded as they lay motionless from exhaustion and pain.

Jim Tomm later learned how the survivors "suffered almost death on the trip from hunger and exposure."[18]

Amazingly, William McIntosh and Jacob Perryman managed to keep their families safely together. Their journey would eventually lead them into Kansas, where they would find refuge with the Union Army at Fort Scott.[19]

Jim Tomm's brother would also make it safely to the military outpost. He and Jacob Perryman were among the scores of freedmen who took up arms with the Union Army.[20]

They would return to Indian Territory in the Spring of 1863 with a newfound sense of freedom and justice. Their return began with the reoccupation of Fort Gibson, prompting Confederate forces to retreat southward.

The two armies would eventually clash July 17, 1863 on the Old Texas Road near a Confederate supply depot at Honey Springs, Indian Territory.

Frank Leslie's Illustrated of the Battle of Honey Springs courtesy of Oklahoma Historical S

From the Darkness / 29

Blood would again flow freely on that day.

Darkness still covered the land when Lucinda awoke on the morning of July 17, 1863, at her family's plantation. Her master's house—a "good log cabin"—sat in a little patch of woods just north of the wagon depot at Honey Springs, and featured an open prairie beyond the front yard that faced north.[21]

A large tree sat in the yard with a swing that dangled from a stout limb on a grape vine.

Lucinda, then a teenager, never forgot that morning.

She was rocking a baby boy named "Istidji" on the swing, passing the time until sunrise. Suddenly, a young rider bolted into the prairie clearing, spurring his horse with the greatest urgency.

Once the rider saw the house he let out a war cry: "Eya-a-a-a-he-ah!"[22]

The rider never broke stride as he galloped passed the house, warning that there was a big battle coming. Lucinda remembered how her "old Master start rapping wid his cane and yelling to git some grub and blankets in de wagon right now!"[23]

Lucinda and the other slaves—mostly women—instantly left everything where it sat and scurried to retrieve the wagons. Fires were doused. Kettles and pots were hoisted into wagons. Mules were harnessed.

A few slaves loaded meat and corn into a wagon,

food that had been hidden from Yankee and Rebel scouts. The motley band then departed on the Old Texas Road in search of a safe haven.

The skies soon opened with a deluge of rain, and before long, the ground ran red with blood.

Lucinda's party passed a large contingent of Confederate soldiers shortly before the first guns were fired. She remembered gazing at a Confederate flag bearer whose horse pitched and reared as the flag whipped in the wind.

"Dey dragging some big guns on wheels and most de men slopping 'long in de rain on foot," Lucinda recalled. "Den we hear de fighting up to de north 'long about whar de river is, and de guns sound lak hosses loping 'cross a plank bridge way off somewar."[24]

A few miles away, Jim Tomm and his family trembled in fear in the crowded cellar beneath a slave cabin. The roar of the cannons and thunder melted together, rattling the cellar door and their nerves. Little did Jim or anyone else in his family know that his brother fighting on the front line in a Yankee uniform.[25]

Dallas W. Bowman, a 19-year-old Confederate soldier, left one of the only eyewitness accounts of the actual battle. Bowman briefly described the scene in a letter to his mother:

> We all were too sure of whipping them but no, we fought over 3 hours under a heavy fire all the time but at last their firing began to get too heavy for us at

the same time dismounting one of our peaces of cannon [.] We were compelled to fall back and our men began to [scatter?], which caused confusion and we had a general stampede, the enemy followed us out to a prairie about a half mile from the battle ground, at which time our Battalion charged on them and held them in check until the train could get out of the way. Our loss was one hundred and thirty...[26]

Union Gen. James G. Blunt reported only 76 casualties, while claiming there were more than 500 Confederate casualties. Confederate Gen. Douglas H. Cooper added to the numbers game by reporting only 181 casualties on his side.

Regardless, the federal troops rightfully laid claim to a huge victory that day and seized the Honey Spring depot. Lucinda and her fellow slaves watched the scene a half mile from the depot from a cave on a high creek embankment.

"We can hear de guns going all day, and along in de evening here come de South side making for a getaway," Lucinda recalled. "Dey come riding and running by whar we is, and it don't make no difference how much de head men hollers at 'em dey can't make dat bunch slow up and stop.

"After while here comes de Yankees, right after 'em, and dey goes on into Honey Springs and pretty soon we see de blaze whar dey is burning de wagon depot and houses."[27]

The Yankees soon reached the Stidham plantation with their torches. They began to set fire to the cabins.

"They came to burn the one over us," Jim Tomm remembered. "We could hear them talk. All of us were scared ..."[28]

Finally, one Yankee soldier yelled, 'Is anybody down in the cellar?' "[29]

Little Jim spoke up from the darkness.

"I'se down heah," he shouted.[30]

This is how freedom entered Jim Tomm's life.

Jim and the other slaves were removed from the cellar, and the cabin was torched. They camped with the Union soldiers that night on Elk Creek. At daybreak, the emancipated slaves were fed, loaded onto three wagons, and escorted under guard on the road back to Fort Gibson.

Bloodied and lifeless bodies lay scattered along the road, and as the caravan passed, the dead Union soldiers were hoisted into piles on wagons. Numerous dead were buried at Fort Gibson, where Jim Tomm was unexpectedly reunited with his older brother among some 1,000 black refugees.[31]

"We met Brother at the fort and by him being with the Northern soldiers, we got good care and plenty to eat," Tomm recalled. "Daddy came back to the Stidham plantation after the war and we all got together again, and not one of the family was killed.

"We sure were lucky."[32]

Revenge on the Long Knives

POWs on top are Mo-chi and Medicine Water, photo from author's collection.

Family oral tradition states *Mo-chi* was buried with all the respect, honor and ceremony befitting a Southern Cheyenne warrior in the spring of 1881. Dressed in the finest buckskins, the 40-year-old fighter was laid to rest on a high, grassy knoll somewhere on the north side of the Lodgepole River (Washita River) in present-day Oklahoma.

Death songs echoed across Indian Territory's western prairie that day as fellow warriors from the once-powerful Bowstring Society sang in *Mo-chi's* honor. Today, the sacred burial site is kept secret.

"And it will remain a secret," said John L. Sipe Jr., *Mo-chi's* great-great grandson. "But it doesn't matter. The Spirit World knows."

By 1881, some American officials viewed *Mo-chi* as a villain. To the Southern Cheyenne, however, *Mo-chi* was a celebrated protector of the people and a warrior of prestige.

What made *Mo-chi* so special? Translated to English, *Mo-chi* means Buffalo Calf Woman.

Mo-chi was one of the few female warriors among the Cheyenne, and perhaps the greatest who ever lived. She rode and fought side-by-side with her husband,

Painting depicts the 7th U.S. Cavalry's attack on the Cheyenne village on the frozen banks of

...ta River in 1868 photo courtesy of Western History Collection, University of Oklahoma

Medicine Water, who was especially notorious among the white settlers during the Staked Plains Wars.

Together, they led several raids against United States soldiers and settlers to protect the Cheyenne homeland. In their wake, they left a path of blood.

Life for *Mo-chi* wasn't always filled with turmoil.

She was born in "Yellowstone Country" of present-day Wyoming around 1841. In time, she learned the ways of her nomadic band as it trailed the mighty buffalo herds across the Great Plains. Memories of her childhood along the North and South Platte rivers were probably pleasant ones. Her mother, grandmothers and aunts taught her how to bead, cook, make cloths with bone awls, butcher meat and tan hides.

Mo-chi grew into a slender, 5-foot-6¾-inch woman with straight black hair and rounded features in her face. She had brown eyes. By the age of 20 she had married a man named Standing Bull.[1]

Whatever peace she knew ended one winter morning in 1864 during the month of the Freezing Moon (November). At dawn on the 29th day, one thousand of the Third Colorado Regiment of Volunteers under the command of Colonel John M. Chivington attacked a camp of some 300 Cheyenne on the banks of the dry-bedded Sand Creek in eastern Colorado Territory.[2]

Cheyenne leaders Black Kettle and White Antelope believed a peace treaty was in effect at the time and had turned in their firearms at nearby Fort Lyon. An American flag given to Black Kettle four years earlier was even hoisted up a long lodgepole outside his lodge—as was a small white flag—as the soldiers approached.[3]

Seconds later, shots pierced the morning stillness as Chivington's troops swooped down on the stunned village. Cheyenne men, women and children were slaughtered indiscriminately.

Yet the *Rocky Mountain News* reported, "Among the brilliant feats of arms in Indian warfare, the recent campaign of our Colorado Volunteers will stand in history with few rivals, and none to exceed in it final results.... A thousand incidents of individual daring and the passing events of the day might be told, but space forbids. We leave the task for eye-witnesses to chronicle. All acquitted themselves well, and Colorado soldiers have again covered themselves in glory."[4]

Another version of the event would later unfold. Chivington's men had choked off the Cheyenne horse herd on the southwestern ridge overlooking the Sand Creek village, causing the Indians to fight where they stood. Many Cheyenne scattered in mass confusion to get their families to safety as the sound of gunfire and screams added to the madness. Sharpshooters picked off a number of Cheyenne people from the surrounding ridge.

Nearby, one band of Arapaho under Chief Left Hand were caught in the onslaught. The few who did not fall, ran for their lives.[5] The volunteer militia were later greeted in the mining boomtown of Denver by

POWs Mo-chi and Medicine Water author's collection

cheering citizens as they displayed the scalps and severed genitals of the Cheyenne like trophies of war.[6]

Major Scott J. Anthony of the First Colorado Calvary would later give testimony on the Sand Creek massacre, relating one unforgettable scene of atrocity:

> There was one little child, probably three years old, just big enough to walk through the sand. The Indians had gone ahead, and this little child was behind following after them. The little fellow was perfectly naked, traveling on the sand. I saw one man get off his horse, at a distance of about seventy-five yards, and draw up his rifle and fire—he missed the child. Another man came up and said, "Let me try the son of a bitch; I can hit him." He got down off his horse, kneeled down and fired at the little child, but he missed him. A third man came up and made a similar remark, and fired, and the little fellow dropped.[7]

Mo-chi darted from her lodge, picking up only a Hawkens rifle that belonged to her father. The rifle was a gift from two trappers he saved during one winter storm on the Bunch of Timber River (Smoky Hill River) in Kansas.[8] She would carry the rifle for most of her remaining days.

On this morning, the 23-year-old *Mo-chi* miraculously carried the rifle and herself to safety by scampering northward along the creek. Late that night as the survivors began to leave the Sand Creek area, she could hear drunken soldiers boasting about their kills.[9]

Mo-chi and the other survivors eventually regrouped along the Bunch of Timber River (Smoky Hill River), and walked to Cherry Creek. It was there they finally reached the fierce Dog Soldiers—one of five independent, Cheyenne war societies—with word of the Sand Creek massacre. Over 137 Indians were killed in the surprise attack. Among the slain were nine Cheyenne peace chiefs. *Mo-chi* lost everyone on her side of the family, including her husband Standing Bull.[10]

Anger spread throughout the Cheyenne camp, and the war pipes were sent to the allied Lakota and Arapaho bands to make war on the whites. The Lakota warriors accepted the war pipes, which meant they would lead the honored charge into battle. For the next 30 days, the Cheyenne healed their wounded on the banks of Cherry Creek and prepared for war.

Shortly before daybreak on January 7, 1865, Lakota warriors led the enraged Cheyenne into the small Colorado settlement of Julesburg, where they made the first of two attacks. A group of soldiers outside Fort Rankin were savagely butchered. Vengeance was so great that day, Cheyenne women and children were even said to have taken part in the retaliation as they burned and plundered Julesburg's warehouses and stores.[11] *Mo-chi* was among the avengers.[12]

Yet the blood did not stop flowing.

Four years later—and two days shy of the Sand Creek anniversary—*Mo-chi* and her extended families

George A. Custer photo from author's collection

were again the targets of an early-morning attack by U.S. troops. This time, the flamboyant Lieutenant Colonel George Armstrong Custer and his 7th Calvalry charged into Black Kettle's sleeping village on the banks of the Lodgepole River (Washita River).

Custer, by his own account, led the charge aboard a magnificent black stallion. He encountered a Cheyenne warrior in the village area who raised his rifle, only to be shot dead by Custer before he could squeeze the trigger. Custer's horse then knocked another Indian to the ground as he headed south to a small knoll, where he watched the rest of the action.[13]

Mo-chi again saw the horrific site of her people being slaughtered as she frantically tried to escape the swarming calvalrymen. Somewhere in the confusion, her three-year-old daughter, Measure Woman, was shot in the hip. The little girl was scooped up and carried to safety. Others were left dead or dying in the snow.

An 18-year-old named Red Bird tried to protect those Cheyenne people crossing the river to the north. He stood in the river and fired at the soldiers before finally being killed himself. One family member glanced back at Red Bird, and saw his big, roan horse rearing up and down at his feet. The relative took aim and shot the horse so that it might join the warrior in the Spirit World.[14]

Over 100 Cheyenne men, women and children may have died in the attack. Black Kettle, who never stopped believing he was at peace with the whites, was among the slain.

Whatever trust that may have still existed for the whites probably vanished from *Mo-chi's* heart that day. The scars of the Sand Creek and Washita attacks cut so deep, in five years time, she would declare an all-out war on the white man. She vowed all white people would pay for their senseless destruction of her people and endless invasion of the Cheyenne homeland.[15]

The rage inside her was probably unleased with the help of her new husband, Medicine Water, who in 1873 became the head war chief of the powerful Bowstring Society. *Mo-chi* proved to be a worthy mate. She rode with Medicine Water and his band for the next two years as they terrorized settlers in Texas, Kansas and the Indian Territory.

Four surveyors on the Many Pipe Dance River (Cimarron River) in Indian Territory became the first of several victims *Mo-chi* and Medicine Water would leave in their wake. These men were killed in March of 1873.

The following year *Mo-chi* and Medicine Water took their open warfare to Adobe Walls on the South Canadian River. The establishment of this Texan outpost was viewed by the Plains Indians as an arrogant gesture, and on June 27, a combined force of some 700 Cheyenne, Comanche and Kiowa attacked the Adobe Walls station. Medicine Water led the charge for the Cheyenne warriors. He was joined by his brothers Iron Shirt and Man On A Cloud.

The Comanche's were guided by the great war Chief Quannah Parker, who was told by a tribal medicine man that none of the attacking Indians would die from the white man's bullets. The medicine would prove bad, as would the surprise attack by the Indians. Drowsy buffalo hunters were awakened in time to punch holes

Custer at Fort Riley, Kansas, courtesy of Western History Collection, University of Oklahoma

through the adobe walls in order to return the fire of the charging Indians. Many warriors, meanwhile, took cover behind mammoth piles of buffalo hides.

Twenty-eight buffalo hunters and one woman miraculously held off each wave of attackers for a full day while trapped inside the adobe station. Several Indians, with hearts swelled by the prophecy of the Comanche medicine man, fearlessly rammed their horses into the doors. But they were quickly shot down by the deadly aim of the buffalo hunters. The legendary stand included Bat Masterson, who later earned fame as a lawman by patrolling some of the meanest cattle towns in the West. Fellow buffalo hunter Billy Dixon would also go down in western lore for his role at Adobe Walls. Dixon reportedly killed a mounted Indian from an estimated 1,250 yards with a .50-90 Sharps rifle.[16]

By the time the gun smoke cleared, countless Indians and three buffalo hunters laid dead.[17]

The fiasco at Adobe Walls further enraged *Mo-chi* and Medicine Water.

Less than one week later, the charred remains of freighter Patrick Hennessey were discovered along the Chisolm Trail in Indian Territory. *Mo-chi*, Medicine Water and sixteen other warriors killed Hennessey and his three companions. Hennessey's remains were found tied to the back two wagon wheels.[18]

Six more surveyors died at the hands of Medicine Water and his band some 60 miles southwest of Dodge

City, Kansas two months later. One surveyor had a compass pounded into his forehead.[19]

Mo-chi and Medicine Water received their greatest notoriety for the September 11, 1874 attack of the German family on the northwestern plains of Kansas.

John German, his wife, Liddia, and their seven children broke camp that morning on the Bunch of Timber River (Smoky Hill River). German, a Civil War veteran from Georgia, had anticipated covering the 15-mile distance along the Butterfield Route to Fort Wallace by nightfall. He and his family then planned to depart Fort Wallace for their final destination—the Colorado Territory.

No one in the family anticipated the nightmare that would follow.

Medicine Water and his warriors swept down on the German's covered wagon with the swiftness of a prairie fire. John German was walking in front of the ox-drawn wagon with a rifle when the Cheyenne attacked. He was the first to die. The 138-pound *Mo-chi* drove an ax into his head.[20]

Nineteen-year-old Stephen was helping his 17-year-old sister, Catherine, round up a small cow herd at the time in a nearby hollow. Stephen was also killed in a matter of moments. Liddia died by her dead husband's side, while her daughters—Rebecca (20) and Joanna (15)—reportedly put up a fight before also being killed. The Cheyenne eventually rode off with four remaining German girls as captives.[21]

Revenge on the Long Knives

The German attack marked the beginning of the end for *Mo-chi* and Medicine Water on the open plains. The German dead were found in early October, at which time a massive manhunt was underway to capture Medicine Water and his hostile band. By then, even *Mo-chi* and Medicine Water were growing tired. Their ponies were thin from the lack of winter grass, and more importantly, they could no longer continue to feed and care for their families who rode with them. They knew their fighting days had to come to an end.

Mo-chi and Medicine Water first considered turning themselves in at the Darlington Agency in Indian Territory while camped on the border of Indian Territory in No Man's Land. Among them was Stone Forehead—Keeper of the Sacred Arrows. The Cheyenne couple thus decided to escort Stone Forehead to safety before laying down their arms.

Wearily, they pressed northward until they reached the safe refuge of the Bunch of Timber River (Smoky Hill River) in Kansas, where they believed the Sacred Arrows would be out of danger. *Mo-chi* and Medicine Water then proceeded back to the Darlington Agency, where they finally surrendered on March 5, 1875.

The Cheyenne avengers would fight no more.

Mo-Chi and Medicine Water were charged with crimes and shipped to Fort Marion, Florida with 30 other Cheyenne warriors as prisoners of war. *Mo-chi* was the lone female prisoner in the group. For six weeks, the Cheyenne POW traveled from Indian

Territory to Fort Marion in chains and shackles. *Mo-chi* and Medicine Water remained in Florida until their release three years later on April 5, 1878.

By that time, the Cheyenne confronted a new fight—one of cultural survival.

Throughout the Great Plains, however, other Cheyenne warriors would carry on the fight for their homelands. In fact, *Mo-chi* would not be the last Cheyenne woman to take up arms against U.S. soldiers. A Northern Cheyenne named Buffalo Calf Road Woman would bring honor to her people on July 17, 1876, at the Battle of the Rosebud. Her brother, Chief Comes In Sight, charged the U.S. troops that day only to have his horse shot down from underneath him.

Buffalo Calf Road Woman suddenly bolted from the Indian ranks, and with enemy Crow scouts charging Chief Comes In Sight, she picked up her brother and rode to safety.[22] Eight days later, she was said to have fought from horseback at Little Bighorn.

Like Buffalo Calf Road Woman, *Mo-chi* said she fought instinctively. Shortly before her death, *Mo-chi* was asked by family members why she rode the warpath. Solemnly, she responded, "I didn't do anything the long knives didn't do to us."[23]

Merciless Frontier

Queton photo from author's collection

Esteban. The name of his birth.

Queton remembered little else about his childhood in Mexico. He often struggled to recall his family's surname, but always to no avail. And over time the names of his mother, father and older brother also vanished with the wind.

The names disappeared just as he did one day, probably in the year 1848.

Queton faintly remembered some of the details from a vantage point somewhere outside Chihuahua City, Mexico ... the dense, black haze hanging over the battlefield ... large ambulances collecting the wounded and dead ... his widowed mother's tears ... his fleeing party's three carros.

Nor did *Queton* ever forget the name *Watch-e-coddy*—his Comanche captor.

Watch-e-coddy personally stole *Queton* from his party during a raid in the aftermath of what was probably the Battle of Sacramento River—a February 28, 1848, Mexican War tussle in which U.S. troops captured Chihuahua City's garrison.

Queton always believed it was in that battle his father died.

Shortly thereafter *Queton* lost the rest of his family

forever. The Comanche raid also netted his mother, two men and two older youths. *Queton* never again saw his older brother whom he presumed either escaped or was slain in the attempt.

The captives were taken to a small, timbered hill where they joined other Comanche warriors and youthful hostages stolen from neighboring villages. Led by a warrior named *Pianavonite* (Big Looking Glass), the raiders and their captives began the large, arduous journey back to the main Comanche village somewhere north of the Rio Grande.

By the next morning *Queton* awoke to discover his mother, the two men and two older youths were gone. He never learned of their fate, only his own.

Queton, roughly five years old at the time, eventually became accepted as a "son" by the *Pianavonite* family after his original captor—*Watch-e-coddy*—declined to claim him. From this incident the tiny Mexican lad was given the name *Queton*, which in the Comanche language can be variously translated as "rejected" or "abandoned."[1]

So went *Queton*'s introduction to life on the frontier.

Queton quickly learned it would be a brutal existence where life was as fleeting as a sunset on the vast, western plains. From these roots *Queton* learned to survive. He learned how to escape death, and how to deliver it whenever necessary.

And the frontier taught him well.

As the years passed *Queton* grew more and more comfortable with the nomadic lifestyle of the Comanche people. Raids and warfare became commonplace. By the fall of 1858—nearly a decade after being stolen from his homeland—he had become well schooled in the ways of a young Comanche warrior and could speak the language fluently.

In October of that fateful year *Queton* lived among the several Comanche bands camped along Rush Creek in Indian Territory (Present-day Grady County, Oklahoma).[2] Generally known at the time as the Wichita Village, the camp stretched for several hundred yards, weaving throughout the numerous ravines and gullies along the creek.

Thick brush and trees partially camouflaged the 120 lodges of the bustling encampment, which also consisted of a contingent of Wichita tribesmen and their thatched huts.[3] By some accounts, the overbearing Comanches had taken control of the Wichita's animals and had practically held them hostage in their own village.[4]

But all was well in the eyes of the Comanches. Or so they thought.

Less than a month earlier Comanche chiefs had negotiated a treaty with American officers at Fort Arbuckle. Calmed by words of peace, the Comanche people settled into their new camp with the accommodating Wichitas to trade and gamble.[5]

Fresh hides were being cured for the coming winter, while women stockpiled food such as ground corn. What *Queton* and his Comanche brethren didn't know, however, was that forces were already in motion on the frontier to again usher violence into their lives.

In July of 1858, Maj. Gen. David Twiggs—the belligerent commander of U.S. troops in Texas—wrote from San Antonio to the Army brass at their West Point, New York headquarters. Twiggs boldly urged his superiors to allow him to initiate an offensive campaign against the hostile Comanches.

The portly Twiggs suggested several companies enter Indian country to hunt the Comanches throughout the coming winter and summer, thus giving them "something to do at home in taking care of their families" so they might "let Texas alone."[6]

Twiggs wanted to punish the Comanches for decades of violent attacks and raids on frontier settlers. He wasn't alone in his desires.

Officers at West Point approved the request.

White encroachment on the Comanche homeland wasn't an issue. On September 15 Capt. Earl Van Dorn of the U.S. Second Cavalry left Fort Belknap in command of a small contingent with orders to attack the Comanches.

Van Dorn crossed the Red River with four companies of the Second Cavalry, one company of the Fifth Infantry, and a force of 135 friendly Waco, Caddo and Tonkawa scouts. They set up a crude, military outpost called Camp Radziminski on the southeast bank of

Otter Creek in present-day Tillman County, Oklahoma—unknowingly 90 miles from the Comanche encampment at the Wichita Village.[7]

Soldiers made the best of their desolate location, immediately constructing small "doghouses" to sleep in and rustic stockades made from the region's light timber. The "doghouses" provided cooler sleeping quarters than the Army-issued tents, and were basically small huts made of mud walls and thatched roofs from tall grass cut along the creek.

But few—if any—slept in peace. The "doghouses" were susceptible to the ashes of the camp's numerous fires and the stockades required constant guard.[8]

Indian scouts, meanwhile, scoured the countryside to locate the whereabouts of the hostile Comanches. Two Wichita scouts—*Nasthoe* (Shot-in-the-Foot) and his son, *Wau-see-sie-an*, traveled east to the Wichita Village where they were stunned to discover several bands of the Comanches camped among their people.

Among the several notable Comanche chiefs present in the village was Buffalo Hump, considered a notorious desperado to Texan settlers and lawmen.

Nasthoe and *Wau-see-sie-an* hid in the brush until nightfall before sneaking into the huts of Wichita chiefs, *Esadowa* and *How-its-cahdle*. The two scouts warned the chiefs of the planned attack on the Comanches, and then vanished in the darkness.

Nasthoe and *Wau-see-sie-an* returned to Camp Radziminski on the afternoon of September 29 to report their findings.[9] Estimates pegged the camp's occupancy near 500 souls. Orders almost instantly filtered down to the soldiers to prepare to ride. Mules, extra horses and supplies were moved into the unfinished stockade, and saddlebags were packed with spare ammunition and food for two days.

Van Dorn expected a short, brutal campaign. And he would soon get what he expected.

As the sun set on a frontier riddled with mesquite, Van Dorn led four cavalry companies and their Indian allies east out of camp toward the Wichita Village. Unaware of any parlay by the Comanche chiefs at Fort Arbuckle, Van Dorn and his troops pressed on throughout the night along the southern rim of the Wichita Mountain range.

Van Dorn prepared his troops for an attack at sunrise. But daybreak came and went without any village in site. Van Dorn demanded answers. He quickly learned the Comanche village was closer to 90 miles from Camp Radziminski rather than the 40 miles reported by his Wichita scouts.

Thus the soldiers forced march unmercifully continued.[10]

By nightfall, the column halted briefly at White Wolf Ford on the southern bank of Medicine Bluff Creek to feed the horses. Soldiers hastily boiled coffee, and then climbed back into their saddles to resume what had become a cumbersome march across the starlit prairie.

From a nearby hilltop a Comanche named *Auti-toy-bitsy* (Brown Young Man) and a band of fellow warriors watched the soldiers as they remounted their horses. They first saw the soldiers near Otter Creek while returning from a raid in Chihuahua, Mexico, and reported what they had seen to the elder chiefs at the Wichita Village. The chiefs asked them to return to the prairie to maintain a vigilance.

Now as they watched the soldiers resume their march they became certain an attack on their village was imminent. Spurring their horses, they dashed back to the village to warn their people.[11]

Excitement spread throughout the encampment at the arrival of the warriors. *Queton*—now a teenager of diminutive stature—mingled among the crowd to find out what had caused the stir. He saw the chiefs of the several bands gather to confer on the matter, and he heard talk of moving the camp and of soldiers coming to attack.

A few villagers feared for the worse and chose to sleep in the nearby brush. Others scoffed at what they were hearing. Weren't the chiefs recently assured of peace by the U.S. officers at Fort Arbuckle? Surely, they argued, the soldiers must be friendly.

Daylight delivered the answer.

Word of a large enemy camp reached Van Dorn while the morning dew still dampened the grass in the undulating valley. A herd of more than 500 ponies grazed on the outskirts of the village.

The cavalrymen moved in unison at hundred-yard intervals with sabers drawn. Finally, through the mist, they saw the Comanche tepees and the Wichita's thatched huts appear amid the trees and brush beyond the creek. A bugle sounded from the left side of the column, prompting the thunderous charge of nearly 225 cavalrymen, their Indian allies and their weary horses.

The Comanche's day of judgment was being delivered by the U.S. Army.

Comanche warriors sprang from their tepees, and presented as Van Dorn later wrote "a warmly defended battle-field."[12] A rain of arrows almost instantly pierced the heavy, powdered smoke from the discharging Army rifles.

One group of warriors made a dash toward the herd so they might fight on horseback, only to discover the horses had already been stampeded by the Army's Tonkawa allies. Delaware and Caddo warriors also plunged into combat, fighting most effectively in skirmishes against the Comanches in the nearby hills and ravines.[13]

Van Dorn personally led three companies into battle at the upper section of the camp, where the main body of Comanches slept. This is where the warriors made their strongest and most desperate stand against the mounted cavalrymen. They were the last line of defense between the soldiers and their retreating families.

One Comanche mother saved her child, *Penateka*, by concealing him in the thick brush.[14]

Queton escaped with similar daring. By now his survival instincts had been sharpened by years of anticipated danger from one Comanche village to the next. He too dove into the brush to avoid the soldiers, and somehow scurried to safety.[15]

The maze of ravines and gullies soon rendered mounted charges impossible, leaving the fate of most to the bloody business of hand-to-hand combat. Brave deeds were remembered on both sides. Perhaps none was remembered with more fervor, however, than the encounter of the Comanche *Mohee* and Lt. James Majors.

The two men were brought together when a group of Comanche women and children tried to escape down a creek branch some 150 yards below the camp.

Lawrence "Sul" Ross, recruiter and commander of the Army's Indian allies, spotted the fleeing party and yelled for help as he rode to cut them off. But only Lt. Cornelius Van Camp, private C.C. Alexander, and a Caddo scout heard his shouts.

At that moment *Mohee* and some 24 other warriors appeared through the smoke to rescue their families. The foursome was trapped. Whirling his horse around, Van Camp raised his double-barreled shotgun to meet the charging warriors. A shower of arrows were unleashed. Van Camp fell from his horse dead, an arrow piercing his heart. Alexander also dropped, severely wounded. In a flash, *Mohee* grabbed Alexander's carbine and shot Ross in the side.

Ross, on summer vacation from Alabama Weslyn College, laid writhing in pain. He could barely move as *Mohee* drew his knife and moved in for the kill. Suddenly, Majors galloped up to intercept *Mohee*. Majors instantly killed the Comanche. Troopers then joined Majors in chasing the rest of the warriors away.[16]

After roughly three hours of fighting the Comanches had been thoroughly defeated and driven from the camp. They suffered heavy losses. Fifty-six warriors laid dead in the field. That total soon climbed to 70. Among the dead were some of their bravest warriors—*Arikarosap* (White Deer), *Tanowine*, and *Auti-toy-bitsy*, the brave who first spotted the soldiers at Otter Creek.[17]

In addition, two Wichitas in the camp were reported as "accidentally killed."[18] They also had their corn crops trampled in the mayhem.

A handful of American soldiers were also added to the list of dead, most prominently being Van Camp—a promising, young officer who was well-liked by his men.[19] Van Dorn himself nearly died at the hands of his enemy. He laid on the battlefield severely wounded from an arrow that passed above his belt and another that penetrated his wrist and passed through his elbow.[20]

While Van Dorn's life remained in serious doubt, his troops set fire to the Comanche's 120 lodges, ammunition, cooking utensils, clothing, dressed skins and food stores. Four days later, a recovering Van Dorn proudly reported to his superiors. He noted that those Comanches who "escaped did so with the scanty clothing they had on and their arms, and nothing was left to mark the site of their camp but the ashes and the dead."[21]

Six days later at Camp Radziminski Van Dorn began entertaining the thought of another expedition against the Comanches. A band had been reported to the north on the Canadian River, where Van Dorn presumed some from the destroyed Wichita Village would find refuge.[22]

Van Dorn may have been right. But a number of Comanches escaped to join the Kiowa people on the Arkansas River. *Queton* was said to be among their lot, and as fate would have it he was sold to a Kiowa family that fall, probably because of the Comanche's scant food supply. Or *Queton* may have been sold at Fort Arbuckle, another refuge for Comanche survivors.

Either way *Queton* wouldn't soon forget the bloody slaughter of the Comanches at the Wichita Village. As an adult he would deliver violence with the same savagery as those who battled at Rush Creek and those who stole him from his homeland.

Ironically, *Queton* rose to become a noted Kiowa warrior. He would engage in the same heartless acts of raiding and fighting, scalping and killing.

On January 12, 1871 *Queton* participated in perhaps his most publicized act of violence when a band of 25 Kiowa warriors cornered three teamsters near Fort

Belknap. Two of the teamsters died quickly, while the third—the celebrated black frontiersman Britt Johnson—made a heroic last stand.

Johnson cut the throat of his horse to use the animal as a breastwork. He then staved off the Kiowas for a time by loading and reloading his gun and those of his dead companions during lulls in the fighting. Johnson's body was later found scalped, mutilated and riddled with 173 cartridge shells.

Years later *Queton* revisited the day Johnson died with an interviewer, laughing how he and his companions playfully tossed the kinky scalps of the black teamsters at one another while riding home. *Queton* told how they eventually tossed the scalps away in disgust because they possessed no value.[23]

The frontier had indeed taught *Queton* well.

Buffalo Wallow Fight

Amos Chapman photo courtesy of the Panhandle Plains Historical Museum.

Amos Chapman's grave sat well beyond the public road, out where the blackjack trees sprouted like weeds and where the land bled into obscurity. There, beneath a mammoth blue prairie sky, the legendary frontier scout was laid to rest after an unceremonious death July 18, 1925, at age 88.

Chapman died in a wagon accident on his homestead four miles outside Seiling, Oklahoma, and was buried in a non-descript plot in the family cemetery.[1]

Yet there was nothing non-descript about Chapman.

The man, like the land, was rugged. He lived a hard life, surviving the Indian Wars and then the arrival of civilization. Through the years his legend grew as big as the vast plains that engulfed his gravesite—a barren patch of red dirt that could carry the observer to that lonely spot in the soul. Chapman would have coveted such a place.

For Chapman feared neither living nor dying.

Col. Richard Irving Dodge could attest to Chapman's courage. Dodge once ranked Chapman among the greatest scouts in American frontier history, placing the Oklahoman in the same lofty company as Kit Carson, California Joe, and "Buffalo" Bill Cody.

"One of the best and bravest, the most sober, quiet and genial of all the scouts I have known is Amos Chapman," Dodge once said. "Although yet young, a volume would scarcely suffice to give all the desperate adventures and hairbreadth escapes of this remarkable man. For 15 years he has been almost constantly employed by the government, and his services and sufferings put him in the front rank of valuable citizens."[2]

Chapman secured his place in the annals of western history in 1874 while employed as a civilian scout and interpreter for the U.S. Army at Camp Supply in Indian Territory. By then, the 37-year-old Chapman had already established himself as a salty veteran of the plains and a crack shot with his rifle.

He would rely on that experience Sept. 12, 1874 in the fight of his life.

War parties of Comanche, Kiowa, and Cheyenne roamed the Texas and Oklahoma plains at the time, having struck a buffalo hunters' camp at Adobe Walls earlier that year with an estimated 700 warriors. For four days in June, 28 men and one woman valiantly defended the outpost and kept their attackers at bay with sharp shooting before the Indians eventually wandered off in either boredom or disgust.[3]

Chapman and fellow scout Billy Dixon—one of the heroes at Adobe Walls—were given orders by Gen. Nelson A. Miles Sept. 10 to carry dispatches from his camp on McClellen Creek in the Texas Panhandle to nearby Fort Supply in Indian Territory. Miles, cam-

Billie Dixon photo courtesy of the Panhandle Plains Historical Museum.

paigning against the marauding Plains Indians, informed the scouts that his command was short on rations.[4]

Miles ordered four enlisted men to accompany Chapman and Dixon—Sergeant. Z.T. Woodhall, and privates John Harrington, Peter Rath, and George W. Smith. He gave them the option of taking more men, but the seasoned scouts knew they would move much swifter with a smaller group.

For the next two days, the small contingent maneuvered across the vast, undulating plains, always resting in secluded spots during daylight. They continued on the morning of Sept 12, ever vigilant of signs of war parties.

Blinding, yellow rays now emerged on the eastern horizon from the sunrise as the small group neared the divide of the Washita River and Gageby Creek. As they crested a knoll, Chapman, Dixon and the soldiers suddenly came face-to-face with about 125 mounted Kiowa and Comanche warriors.

Horses were jerked to a halt. Mists of white clouds puffed from the nostrils of every horse for one frozen moment. Suddenly, the world moved at a blinding pace.

The Indians reacted almost instantaneously, erupting in yells and circling a ring around the tiny group. Guns blazed.[5]

"We knew the best thing to do was to make a stand and fight for our lives, as there would be great danger of our becoming separated in the excitement of a running fight, after which the Indians could more easily kill us one by one," Dixon would later write. "We also realized that we could do better work on foot; as we dismounted and placed our horses in the care of George Smith."[6]

A shot soon pierced Smith's breast and he fell face down, sending the horses stampeding in every direction. The horses quickly vanished in the chaos, carrying with them any additional clothing and all rations of food and water.

The shootout continued at close range—close enough to peer into the enemy's desperate eyes. Dixon would later notice that his thin, cashmere shirt had been pierced several times by bullets that never struck flesh. He suffered a lone shot to one calf, but still managed to work off adrenaline and the fear of being captured.

Dixon and his companions knew they would undergo a gruesome torture and death if captured alive. Frantically, knowing they were one full rush from being overtaken, they canvassed the terrain for a spot to make their final stand.

A mesquite flat several hundred yards away caught their eyes. Together, they agreed to make a desperate break for that area in hopes it would provide them with enough cover to survive.

Just then a bullet ripped into Chapman. It shattered his left knee.

"Billy," Chapman said as he slowly sank to the dirt, "I am hit at last."[7]

Now every white defender, save for Rath and Dixon, had been severely wounded. Realizing their situation was growing more and more dire, Dixon desperately scanned the terrain once again, never ceasing to discharge his gun.

This time Dixon spotted a "buffalo wallow," a slight depression in the ground made by buffalo as they paw and wallow in a spot. Dixon sprinted for the wallow in a hail of gunfire. Bullets buzzed his ears.[8]

Sliding into the wallow, Dixon quickly noticed it to be about 10 feet in diameter with enough depth to provide some protection. He shouted for his comrades to join him, and instantly each made their own dash while firing their guns. Dixon provided cover with a constant fire. All, except for Chapman and Smith, made it safely to the wallow.

No one even knew whether Smith was still alive. He lay motionless with his face buried in the dirt.

The men in the wallow desperately stabbed at the earth, flinging the sandy dirt up around them to build a crude barricade. From time to time, they stopped digging in order to return gunfire against a charging Indian.

The Indian yell echoed long after the discharge of the firearm, hanging in the air and mind. Knuckles went white against the six-shooter whenever an Indian charged with his spear raised in a cocked position.

"Many times that terrible day did I think that my last moment was at hand," Dixon later recalled. "We were keenly aware that the only thing to do was to sell our lives as dearly as possible. We fired deliberately, taking good aim, and were picking off Indians at almost every round."[9]

Chapman lay incapacitated in the open.

A voice from the wallow called out for Chapman,

urging him to hobble over to them. Chapman said he couldn't. His leg had been shattered above one knee.

"You boys keep me covered and I'll try to get him," Dixon shouts.[10]

"Hell, you'll get your hide full of holes!" one replied. "Don't do it!"[11]

Dixon sprang from the wallow anyway to drag his friend to safety, but was repelled by a volley of gunfire from the circling Indians. He made one attempt after another until finally reaching Chapman.

"Quick," Dixon shouted to Chapman, "climb onto my back."[12]

Chapman latched onto Dixon's back. The weight of the bigger Chapman buckled Dixon's knees as he plodded and stumbled back the wallow. Chapman shrieked in pain. Bullets whistled past them like swarming bees.

Somehow they made it back to the wallow untouched.

"Damned good job, Billy," Chapman said as Dixon gasped for breath. "Thanks. Gimme a gun!"[13]

Thoughts quickly turned to Smith, but each agreed it would be foolish to risk retrieving a dead man's body under such dangerous circumstances. Smith showed no signs of life since being dropped in the opening salvos.

Dig, they thought out loud. Dig.

Clawing at the sandy soil with their fingers and knifes, they managed to shovel more and more dirt up around them. They literally dug for their lives.

Bullets pelted the dirt around them, sending puffs of red dirt floating into the air. Occasionally, an Indian thirsty for glory would ride headlong toward the entrenched men at top speed, only to be shot from his mount.

The charges became less frequent.

So did the firing from the wallow. The men knew they could only live as long as their ammunition lasted. Every shot would have to count.

The men now faced another foreboding challenge. They were desperately thirsty.

No one really noticed in the angst of the gunfight. Who had time to notice? But as the Indians withdrew to safer ground, each defender became highly aware their water had ridden away with their bolting mounts at the outset of the fight. Tongues swelled, sticking to parched mouths that no longer produced saliva.

The situation was dire.

Just then Chapman and Dixon looked to the western sky, where black, billowing clouds swirled as ominously as the Indians who desired their scalps. Before long, thunder rocked the land, lightning lit up the sky, and sheets of rain pelted the landscape. The downpour came so fast and furious it filled the buffalo wallow quickly, leaving the men drenched in a large puddle of water.

The relief was nonetheless embraced by these desperate men, who instinctively bent down and sucked down large gulps of water that now ran red with their own blood.

No one cared.

Then the elements ushered in another cruelty when the winds shifted to the north. The wind and rain turned cold, chilling the men to the bone. Like their supply of water, their coats and additional clothing were tied to their horses, which now wandered the plains.

Teeth began to chatter. The men trembled from the cold, but never complained. They were, at least for a time, still alive. Or at least most of them were. Smith still lay motionless outside the wallow, face down in what was now slushy mud.

Someone turned attention to the ammunition supply. Each realized their chance for survival would last only as long as their ammunition. Shots were now fired only if an Indian approached in a direct charge.

One man pointed to Smith's belt and six-shooter, reasoning it was probably still full since he fell during the opening salvos of the fight. Only now, under the cover of darkness and with Indians shivering themselves from the rain, did the recovery of Smith's weapon become reasonable.

Rath, the only defender beside Dixon to avoid serious injury thus far, volunteered to retrieve the six-shooter. He raced to Smith's side and paused for a moment before racing back to the wallow.

The Indians watched silently as they sat on their

mounts. They too shivered, huddling beneath their blankets.

"Smith is still alive!" Rath excitedly explained.[14]

Chapman and his comrades were astonished by the news. Dixon immediately accompanied Rath outside the wallow to retrieve the unfortunate Smith, who had been shot in the left lung. Whenever he breathed the wind exited his back, just below his shoulder blade, in a bloody mist. He was as good as dead, and there was a sense of guilt shared by all the men who had given him up for dead.

Still, there was nothing that could really be done for him.

Dixon and Rath hurriedly carried him back to the wallow, carefully laying him down against the edge of the dirt embankment. Smith moaned pitifully. Dixon grabbed a stiff willow switch, which lay nearby and had been dropped by a charging Indian. The willow had been used to whip the Indian's horse, but Dixon now folded a silk handkerchief over the willow, and stuffed into the bullet hole in Smith's back.

Smith moaned once more.

The men now huddled together, although it wasn't enough to dull the sting of the bitter cold. The wind whipped mercilessly, and hunger began to take hold. Sleep, naturally, was out of the question. So they waited and peered into the darkness, thankful for every minute the Indians kept their distance.

Dixon thought about gathering some grass for bedding, anything really that would put something dry between them and the wet ground. But the Indians had scorched the entire countryside until it became blackened and nearly barren. Dixon and Rath quickly deduced they could instead gather some tumbleweed.

The men poked around in darkness, covered by a sliver of moonlight and never straying far from the wallow. They succeeded in gathering enough tumbleweed to crush and lay beneath them—a supply Dixon equated to the "spring of a wire mattress."[15]

Dixon again turned his attention to their firearms. He grabbed a willow, and began the menial, yet necessary task of cleaning each barrel. The busier he remained, the less he pondered his final fallback plan.

He secretly determined to "save my last bullet for my self-destruction." It was a thought they all shared, yet went unspoken.[16]

For deep down, where men dig for courage, each found a flickering light of hope. That hope, they concluded unanimously, rested in a desperate flight by one of their lot to retrieve help.

Dixon felt he had the best chance of maneuvering across the Plains and finding help if he made it out alive. He knew the terrain as well, if not better than Chapman, who was in no shape to walk. Dixon thus volunteered to go, but the others quickly balked at the notion. His marksmanship, they contended, would be needed to keep the hostiles at bay.

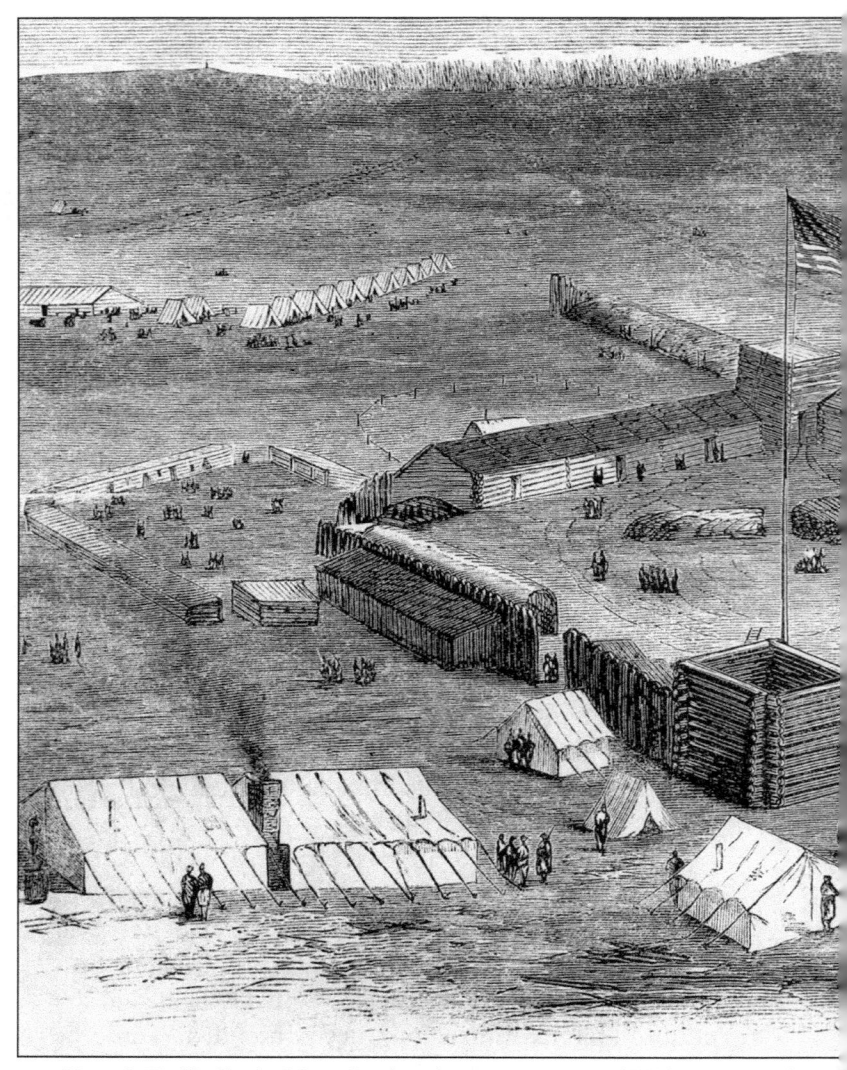

Harper's Weekly *Sketch of Camp Supply, Indian Territory courtesy of Oklahoma Historical Society*

Buffalo Wallow Fight / 83

Dixon grabbed his gun to leave, only to be drawn back by the protests of the wounded. He abandoned the idea against his better judgment, and Rath was elected for the daring duty.

Staring at the dying Smith and wounded Chapman, who clutched his shattered leg, Rath bid them goodbye and disappeared into the night.

Rath returned about two hours later. He couldn't find the trail.

The wind moaned woefully.

By then, Smith groaned pitifully and begged for someone to end his suffering. He repeatedly asked to be shot. The five other men felt helpless, as if they were adrift on the ocean aboard nothing more than a raft. They tried to make Smith comfortable, for all knew his fate had been sealed.

Later that night, Smith drifted off to sleep and then mercifully into eternity. Someone felt his pulse. None existed. He was cold and stiff.

Gently, the five survivors lifted Smith's body outside of the wallow onto a skimpy bed of mesquite grass. A white handkerchief was placed over his face.

The men again huddled together to combat the cold, gripping their firearms. Dixon thought often of the butcher knife that hung at his side. He always kept the blade razor sharp, and considered cutting his long hair more than once.

Indian warriors coveted scalps with long hair. Morbid thoughts visited each man that night as visions of another Indian attack raged in their minds. They guarded every moment as if it might be their last.

By daybreak, the group agreed to let Dixon go for help. The Indians were nowhere in sight. So Dixon wasted no time in making his escape, although the daylight now exposed him to greater danger. Travelers in that region could literally be seen for miles.

Odds of eluding an approaching band of Indians would be slim.

Within minutes, Dixon found the trail that led to Camp Supply. He moved briskly, weaving in and out of cover wherever it existed. His eyes darted about the terrain for Indians.

Suddenly, his eyes caught the approach of many riders, enough to cover an acre of land. Dixon scurried for a thicket of tall grass. He waited and waited. His heart pounded. Tired and desperate for an answer, Dixon poked his head out for another look.

The riders rode abreast.

"Shortly I was able to see that they were troops," Dixon said. "Indians always traveled strung out in a line ... I never felt happier in my life."[17]

Dixon fired his rifle in the sky. The troops lurched to a halt. Dixon fired again.

Two soldiers rode toward him. Soon, they were listening to Dixon's harrowing account and the whereabouts of his besieged comrades.

The soldiers belonged with the 8th U.S. Cavalry under the command of Maj. William R. Price, who was escorting Gen. Miles' supply train from Camp Supply. The supply train, under the command of Capt. Wyllys Lyman, had been trapped for four days on the Washita River by a large contingent of warring Indians.

Price's command freed Lyman's group and ran off the Indians—a hostile force that would later stumble upon Dixon's small party.

Price ordered his surgeon and a relief party to aid the besieged men, who were out of sight but only about a mile away. He asked Dixon to remain behind to give him details of their desperate fight.

Dixon agreed, telling the surgeon where his comrades could be found. As the relief force approached the buffalo wallow, the jittery survivors fired on them, assuming they were Indians. Alarmed, Dixon ran as fast as he could to his friends, hoping he wouldn't be shot in the process.

Chapman and the other survivors recognized Dixon and gleefully lowered their weapons. The wounded men were soon being tending to by the surgeon, and were ripping into the hardtack and dried beef given to them by the soldiers.

Amazingly, Price ordered his men to continue toward Miles without the five survivors—a decision for which he would later be severely reprimanded. Price even declined to leave behind additional firearms and ammunition, but said he would inform Miles of their condition and whereabouts.

Chapman, Dixon, Harrington, Rath, and Woodhall

were suddenly staring at another anxious night on the Plains, haunted by the realization they remained a crippled, exposed target should the Indians return. Furthermore, they had nearly exhausted their ammunition.

Still, they clung to the hope Miles would ride to their rescue the minute he heard the news.

The wind continued to whip the barren landscape throughout the day, perhaps the longest day of their lives. Eventually they again found themselves covered by darkness and leery of a sneak attack.

Then, above the lonely moan of the wind, they heard the faint, yet distinct sound of a bugle. The sound grew louder and louder.

"It made us swallow a big lump in our throats and bite our lips," Dixon would recall years later. "Nearer and clearer came the bugle notes. Our nerves were getting 'jumpy,' so strong was our emotion. We fired our guns, to let them know where we were, and soon the soldiers came riding out of the darkness."[18]

Before leaving the scene of their desperate struggle, the men wrapped Smith in an Army blanket and bury him in the wallow. The soldiers then helped the party to the nearby creek, where they cooked them a meal. The group was eventually escorted to Camp Supply.

Harrington and Woodhall would recover fully from their wounds.

Surgeons amputated Chapman's left leg above the knee. Chapman—whom Dixon claimed was "as tough as second growth hickory"— continued to serve as post interpreter with an artificial leg, riding a horse with the same skill and confidence as he did prior to the Buffalo Wallow Fight.[19]

General Miles, meanwhile, would memorialize the bravery of the besieged in an official correspondence while camped on the Washita River in Texas. On Sept. 24, 1874, Miles wrote:

> "I deem it but a duty to brave men and faithful soldiers to bring to the notice of the highest military authority an instance of the indomitable courage, skill and true heroism on the part of a detachment from his command, with the request that the actors be rewarded, and their faithfulness and bravery be recognized by pensions, medals of honor, or in such way as may be deemed most fitting.
>
> "On the night of the 10th instant, a party consisting of Sergeant Z.T. Woodhall, Co. 'I,' Privates Peter Rath, Co. 'A,' John Harrington, Co. 'H,' and George W. Smith, Co. 'M,' 6th Cavalry, and Scouts Amos Chapman and William Dixon, were sent as bearers of Dispatches from the Camp of this command on McClellan Creek, Texas, to Camp Supply, I.T.
>
> "At 6 a.m. of the 12th, when approaching the Washita River, they were met and surrounded by a band of about 125 Kiowas and Comanches, who had recently left their agency, and at the first attack four of the six were struck. Pvt. Smith, mortally, and the three others severely wounded. Although enclosed on all sides and by overwhelming numbers, one of them succeeded, while they were under a severe fire

at short range, and while others with their rifles were keeping the Indians at bay, in digging with his knife and hands a light cover. After this had been secured they placed themselves within it, the wounded walking with brave and painful efforts, and Private Smith—though he had received a mortal wound—sitting upright in the trench, to conceal the crippled condition of their party from the Indians.

"From early morning till dark, outnumbered 25 to 1, under an almost constant fire and at such short range that they sometimes used their pistols, retaining the last charge to prevent capture and torture, this little party of five defended their lives and the person of their dying comrade, without food, and their only drink the rain water that collected in a pool mingled with their own blood.

"There is no doubt but that they killed more than double their number, besides those that were wounded. The Indians abandoned the attack on the 12th at dark.

"The exposure and distance from the command, which were necessary incidents of their duty, were such, that for thirty-six hours from the first attack, their condition could not be known, and not til midnight of the 13th could they receive medical attendance and food, exposed during this time to an incessant cold storm.

"Sergt. Woodhall, Private Harrington and Scout Chapman were seriously wounded. Private Smith died of his wounds on the morning of the 13th. Private Rath and Scout Dixon were struck but not disabled.

"The simple recital of their deeds, and the mention of the odds against which they fought, how the wounded defended the dying, and the dying aided the wounded by exposure to fresh wounds after the power of action was gone, these alone present a scene of cool courage, heroism and self-sacrifice, which duty, as well as inclination, prompts us to recognize, but which we cannot fitly honor."[20]

Recognition came in the form of the Congressional Medal of Honor, but the award would later be revoked for Dixon and Chapman because of their civilian status. The U.S. Army restored the medals in 1989, long after the scouts had faded into eternity.[21]

Dixon, like Chapman, spent his final years in the open spaces of Oklahoma at his Cimarron County homestead. He was reportedly living in poverty when he died March 9, 1913 of pneumonia. Members of his Masonic Lodge buried him in a cemetery at Texline, but his remains were re-interred 16 years later at the Adobe Walls site where he first became a hero.[22]

Chapman lived his final days in peace with his Cheyenne wife, Mary Longneck. Legend said they "divided matters evenly" at their Oklahoma ranch, sometimes even sleeping in a tepee. Chapman was reportedly preparing for a lecture tour of his frontier days at the time of his death.[23]

Both men were forever bonded by those courageous hours in the buffalo wallow.

A year after his death, Dixon's memoirs were published by his wife, Olive. Dixon was quoted as saying, "I should like once more to meet the men with whom I fought in the Buffalo Wallow Fight, but I seldom hear from them."[24]

Dixon never got his wish. He and his comrades were instead left with the memories of their desperate struggle for life—memories that never failed to stir their blood. Their deeds in the buffalo wallow are now entrenched in the realm of legend, far beyond any monument or non-descript grave.

For in their moment of truth, when life teetered on eternity, they were prepared to die for each other. In doing so, they discovered the gift of life and the thrill of living.

Oklahoma History Timeline

1803
President Thomas Jefferson acquires Oklahoma as part of the Louisiana Purchase for $15 million from France.

1824
Fort Gibson and Fort Towson are established.

1828
The Cherokees of Georgia sign a treaty with the U.S. government, agreeing to move on reservation of seven million acres west of Arkansas, beginning what would later become known as the "Trail of Tears." In time, the Chickasaw, Choctaw, Creek, and Seminole people would be encouraged and then forced to join the Cherokee. Thousands of American Indians would die on the bloody marches into Oklahoma.

1830
The U.S. Congress passes an act that creates Indian Territory.

1833
War breaks out between the Osage and Kiowa. A

defining episode in the conflict occurs that summer when an Osage war party swoops into a Kiowa village on the western rim of the Wichita Mountains and killed 150 Kiowa. Many of the Kiowa warriors are absent at the time of the attack. When they return, they discovered the severed heads of friends and loved ones sitting in metal buckets once obtained from white traders. The site became known as Cutthroat Gap.

1842

Fort Washita is established.

1845

Texas is annexed by the United States. The panhandle—"No Man's Land"—is included in Texas lands.

1850

Texas relinquishes the land that encompasses the so-called "No Man's Land" as the bounds for New Mexico Territory are established. "No Man's Land" is unattached to any state, territory, or Indian reservation.

1851

Fort Arbuckle is established.

1852

Captain R.B. Marcy leads a surveying and exploring expedition along the Red River. He mistakes the North Fork of the Red River as the Red River, thus setting in motion future disputes over Greer County between Texas and Oklahoma.

1859
Fort Cobb is established.

1861
The Choctaw, Chickasaw, Creek, and Seminole nations declare allegiance to the Confederacy. Fort Arbuckle, Fort Cobb, and Fort Washita are abandoned by Union forces, and the Indian Territory is declared under military control of the Confederate Army May 13.

1863
Union troops under Gen. James G. Blunt rout Confederate troops under Gen. Douglas H. Cooper July 17 in the Battle of Honey Springs near present-day Rentiesville. The battle played a key role in Union forces taking control of Indian Territory. Another unique aspect of this engagement is that white soldiers were a minority on both sides. Indians and blacks made up the majority of the soldiers of the opposing armies.

1867
Cattlemen begin driving cattle from southern Texas across the Red River to Abilene, Kansas in what would become known as the Chisholm Trail. The trail is used until 1884 to drive cattle to the railhead of the Kansas

Pacific Railway, where they are shipped eastward. The trail is named after Jesse Chisholm who built several trading posts prior to the Civil War in what would become western Oklahoma. Ironically, Chisholm never drove cattle on the trail. He died in 1868.

1868

Lt. Col. George Armstrong Custer and the 7th Cavalry attack a sleeping Cheyenne village on the frozen banks of the Washita River in present-day Roger Mills County. Over 100 Cheyenne men, women, and children are killed, along with Chief Black Kettle—a peace chief who flew an American flag outside his tepee.

Camp Supply is established. In December 1878, name of post is officially changed to Fort Supply.

1869

Fort Sill is established.

1870

The Missouri, Kansas, and Texas Railroad begins laying tracks into Indian Territory.

1874

Bands of Kiowa, Comanche, Cheyenne, and Arapaho go on the warpath, signaling the last great outbreak on the plains. Peace is restored a year later after much bloodshed.

1875

Fort Reno is established.

The first cattle ranches are opened on the western prairie of Indian Territory.

Comanche Chief Quanah Parker surrenders at Fort Sill. Parker is a noted warrior who led the attack on the buffalo hunters at Adobe Walls in the Texas Panhandle. Cynthia Ann Parker, Quanah's mother, was kidnapped as a child by Comanche raiders in 1836 in Texas. She lived among the Comanche people, and eventually gave birth to Quanah sometime in 1845. Later in life, Quanah's mixed blood and prestige allow him to help bridge the gap between the Comanche people and the U.S. government officials.

1879

William Penn Adair "Will" Rogers is born Nov. 4 on the Dog Iron Ranch in Indian Territory. Rogers would become world renown as a comedian, humorist, social commentator, vaudeville performer, and actor. Rogers, who openly acknowledged his Cherokee heritage, once quipped, "My ancestors didn't come over on the Mayflower, but they met the boat." Rogers died Aug. 15, 1935 in a plane crash with renown Oklahoma aviator Wiley Post in Alaska.

1880

Myra Maybelle Shirley, popularly known as female bandit Belle Starr, marries Cherokee Sam Starr and settles on Starr family land in Indian Territory. Belle Starr is murdered Feb. 3, 1889—a homicide that remains unsolved. Her life, as her death, is wrapped in myth.

1887

Jim Thorpe is born May 28 in Prague, Oklahoma. Thorpe grows up to become perhaps the greatest all-around athlete in American sports history. Thorpe wins gold medals in the 1912 Olympics in the decathlon and pentathlon. He also emerges as a standout in professional football and baseball.

1889

Oklahoma lands are opened by a presidential proclamation, and more than 50,000 people race to stake their claims at high noon April 22. Oklahoma City and Guthrie pop up overnight.

1891

President Benjamin Harrison declares that at noon Sept. 22 the surplus lands of the Sac and Fox, Iowa, Pottawatomie, and Absentee Shawnee reservations east of the original land run are opened for settlement.

1892

The Cheyenne-Arapaho Land Run takes place

April 19 as settlers race to stake claims on more than 3.5 million acres in western Oklahoma Territory

Cherokee outlaw Ned Christie is shot dead by a posse outside his home in present-day Adair County.

1893

Settlers race for land Sept. 16 at noon in the Cherokee Outlet in the largest and perhaps most spectacular of all Oklahoma land runs.

Apache war leader Geronimo and other prisoners of war arrive at Fort Sill Oct. 4 after several years of captivity at Fort Pickens, Florida; and Mount Vernon Barracks, Alabama. Geronimo arrives to angry Oklahomans who decry him as a "murderer." Seven years earlier, on Sept. 5, 1886, the nation rejoiced at the news Geronimo had surrendered to Brig. Gen. Nelson A. Miles. Geronimo and a small band of holdouts had eluded a force of 5,000 regular U.S. Army troops prior to their surrender. Geronimo died Feb. 17, 1909 of pneumonia, and was buried in an Apache cemetery near Cache Creek. Rumors later circulated that Geronimo's relatives secreted his remains away to another location.

The Dawes Commission is authorized under a rider to an Indian Office appropriation bill March 3 with the purpose of convincing the Five Civilized Tribes to cede tribal lands in exchange for individual allotments. This created the Dawes Rolls, now a main source for genealogists tracing their family roots. The rolls are fraught with omissions since Indian enrollees with mixed tribal heritage could only list one tribe. Freedmen, or former slaves, were also served an injustice at this time because they were kept off the rolls despite, in many cases, being considered a member of their respective tribes.

1896

Greer County, Texas is made part of Oklahoma by an act of the U.S. Congress May 4.

1901

The Federal Land Lottery begins July 29 for land in the Lawton district and El Reno district. For several days, the names of the fortunate are published in Oklahoma newspapers, as well as newspapers in surrounding states. Some 11,638 lucky homesteaders are notified, many of whom are later disqualified for various reasons. The lottery is generally considered a success over the "horse race" plan that spawned a wave of "Sooners" who illegally entered the designated territories before the law allowed.

1905

President Theodore Roosevelt visits Frederick, Oklahoma Territory to take part in a wolf hunt with Jack "Catch 'Em Alive" Abernathy and Comanche Chief Quanah Parker. Abernathy is a local legend, noted for catching wolves with his bare hands.

Abernathy didn't disappoint. Roosevelt was so impressed he had part of the hunt filmed so he would have proof of Abernathy's amazing feat for friends back in Washington, D.C. Roosevelt promises make Oklahoma a state.

1907

The Wichita Mountains Wildlife Refuge is established near Lawton—a 59,000-acre reserve for buffalo, longhorn, elk, and whitetail deer.

Bass Reeves retires after 32 years as a federal peace officer, having arrested more than 4,000 felons. He is one of the first Black Americans commissioned as a U.S. Marshall west of the Mississippi River. Reeves became legendary for his work in Indian Territory, where he served Judge Isaac C. Parker of Fort Smith, Arkansas. At statehood, he became a member of the Muskogee, Oklahoma police department. He died in 1910 at age 72.

Indian Territory and Oklahoma Territory are combined Nov. 16 to create the new state of Oklahoma—the 46th state in the Union. President Roosevelt keeps his promise to Oklahomans.

Endnotes

Summer of Sorrow

1. Jack Haley interview with author, 20 May 1999, Roosevelt, Oklahoma. Haley's informant was of course Hunting Horse, whom he distinctly remembered as being "a great orator" and having "great eyesight even at that advanced age." Haley was born July 4, 1931, on the Comanche County, Oklahoma, ranch where he now lives. The ranch is located roughly two miles southeast of Cooperton. Part of Haley's land includes the site where an Osage war party attacked a Kiowa village in 1833. The encounter has become popularly known as the Cutthroat Gap Massacre.

2. Mooney, James. *Calendar History of the Kiowa Indians: Seventeenth-Annual Report Of The Bureau Of American Ethnology* (Washinton: Government Printers Office, 1898), 257. Mooney interviewed a few survivors and a number of Kiowa elders for his report, which is considered the best source on the event.

3. Nye, Wilbur S. *Carbine and Lance* (Norman: University of Oklahoma Press, 1937), 5. Part of the earthen remains of this crude defense are reportedly still visible on the south bank of the Washita River, roughly one-half mile west of the mouth of Rainy Mountain Creek near the present-day town of Mountain View, Oklahoma.

4. Haley interview with author. Haley said he has been told by Kiowa informants that the wild blackberries and plums were in season. If so, he thinks this would place the time of encampment about June.

5. Haley interview with author.

6. Corwin, Hugh D. *The Kiowa Indians: Their History and Life Stories* (Lawton, 1958), 18.

7. Nye, *Carbine and Lance*, 6. Nye noted his informants as Frank

Given and *Ay-tah*, whose grandfather was the boy who ran to give the alarm. Given, the son of *Satank*, was told of the boy from Calf Mountain, a survivor of the massacre.

8. Ibid.

9. Mooney, *Calendar History*, 259; Nye, *Carbine and Lance*, 6.

10. Mooney, *Calendar History*, 258.

11. Ernest Toppah interview with author, 10 May 1999. Toppah grew up hearing stories about the massacre at Cutthroat Gap from his grandfather, Harry Hall. Today Toppah works at the Kiowa's tribal historian; Haley interview with author, concerning the women who died in defense of their children.

12. Mooney, *Calendar History*, 258.

13. Ibid.

14. Haley, Jack. "Cutthroat Gap Massacre," *The War Chief of The Indian Territory Posse of Oklahoma Westerners* (Vol. 13, No. 4, March 1980).

15. *The Chronicles of Oklahoma* (Vol. 45, No. 4, Winter 1967-1968), 474. In a taped narration of the "Story of Cutthroat Gap Massacre, 1833" recorded at the massacre site on October 6, 1993, Kiowa elder Atwater Onco says the boy carried to safety by the father shooting arrows was Stumbling Bear. This account can't be discounted. Onco was born in 1931, and personally heard stories about Cutthroat Gap from elders like Hunting Horse and Andrew Stumbling Bear.

16. Corwin, *The Kiowa Indians*, 21. Corwin obtained his information from Kiowa elders Beulah Hall, *Tine-yu-yah* and Moses Poolaw. Corwin also noted the Cheyennes "trailed the (Osage) war party as far as where Richards Spur is now located."

17. Mooney, *Calendar History*, 259; Nye, *Carbine and Lance*, 7; Topah interview with author. According to Topah, his grandfather told him the Osage used sharpened buffalo ribs to cut the heads of their Kiowa victims. One of the buckets allegedly used by the Osage is on display at the Fort Sill Museum. The now-blackened and dented bucket was presented by George Hunt, who received it from *Ah-vo-ty*, the wife of Stumbling Bear (Corwin, *The Kiowa Indians*, 21). Another bucket is said to be in the private possession of an unidentified Kiowa family (Haley interview with author).

18. Haley interview with author.
Mooney, *Calendar History*, 259.

19. Ibid; Haley interview with author. Hunting Horse told Haley where his mother told him of the mass grave's general location. A granite marker on the ridge above that location serves as a memoril to the victims of the massacre. As for the exact location of the grave, Haley figures that is best kept a secret.

20. Gene Geionety interview with author, 15 September 1999, Carnegie, Oklahoma. Geionety was told the story as a young man from his grandfather, George Geionety. The little girl who survived the massacre was his fourth-great grandmother whose name is unknown. Her son was known simply as Old Man Geionety.

21. Catlin, George. *Letters and Notes of the Manners, Customs, and Condition of the North American Indians* (London: 1841), 75.

22. Mooney, *Calendar History*, 259.

From the Darkness

1. Jim Tomm interview with Works Progress Administration field worker L.W. Wilson in April 1937 in Muskogee, Oklahoma. A transcript of that interview can be found in the *Indian and Pioneer History*, Grant Foreman Collection, v 112, 277-305, Archives Division, Oklahoma Historical Society.

2. Ibid., 283.

3. Ibid., 279.

4. Ibid., 280.

5. Ibid., 278-279.

6. Ibid., 279.

7. *The Oklahoman*, 4 February, 2001.

8. Ibid.

9. For a thorough, no-nonsense treatment of this crucial moment in Oklahoma history see Mary Jane Warde's article "Now the Wolf Has Come: The Civilian War in the Indian Territory," *Chronicles of Oklahoma* (1993), v. 71, 64-87.

10. Opothleyahola and Ouktahnaserharjo letter to "The President our Great Father," February 15, 1861, quoted in Annie Heloise Abel's *The American Indian as Slaveholder and Secessionist: An*

Omitted Chapter in the Diplomatic History of the Southern Confederacy (Cleveland: Arthur H. Clark Company, 1915), 245-246.

11. Tomm interview, 283.
12. Ibid., 282; Baker, T. Lindsay and Baker, Julie P. Baker, ed. *The WPA Oklahoma Slave Narratives*, (Norman, University of Oklahoma Press, 1996), 112. Former slave Lucinda Davis of Tulsa was interviewed by a WPA field worker in 1937. She grew up near the Honey Springs battlefield, and remembered the exodus of slaves from Creek Nation plantations at the outbreak of the Civil War. "Jest de women was all dat was left, 'cause de men slaves had all slipped off and left out," Davis recalled.
13. *The WPA Slave Narratives*, 31.
14. Ibid. Former slave Phoebe Banks was interviewed during the winter of 1937-1938 by WPA field worker Ethel Wolfe Garrison in Muskogee, Oklahoma. Banks said she was born Oct. 17, 1860, and was owned by Mose Perryman.
15. Ibid.
16. Ibid.
17. Ibid.
18. Tomm interview, 281.
19. William McIntosh would shortly thereafter go to work at the Fort Scott blacksmith shop, while Jacob Perryman would join the Union Army. He was later stationed at Fort Gibson, Indian Territory, and fought with Union forces at the Battle of Honey Springs.
20. Tomm interview, 282; *The WPA Slave Narratives*, 32.
21. *The WPA Slaves Narratives*, 109, 112. Former slave Lucinda Davis was interviewed in the summer of 1937 by WPA field worker Robert Vinson Lackey in Tulsa, Oklahoma. Davis' age at the time was listed at "about" 78. "I don't know where I been born," Davis told Lackey. "Nobody never did tell me."
22. Ibid., 112.
23. Ibid.
24. Ibid., 113.
25. Tomm interview, 283.
26. Dallas W. Bowman letter to "Dear Mother," 16 August, 1863, Camp Cooper, Creek Nation, Dallas W. Bowman Papers,

Archives Division, Oklahoma Historical Society. Bowman married Catherine McKinney—a Choctaw woman—in 1864 and remained in Indian Territory after the war, living somewhere on or near the Kiamichi Mountains. The couple had one son, Edward Spencer, who was born in September 1865. Dallas reportedly died in January 1869—one month after his wife's death.

27. *The WPA Slave Narratives*, 113.
28. Tomm interview, 283.
29. Ibid.
30. Ibid., 283-284.
31. Ibid., 284.
32. Ibid., 285.

Revenge on the Long Knives

1. John L. Sipe Jr., interview with author, 7 October 1996. Oral evidence for this article was presented by Sipe Jr., the great-great grandson of Mo-Chi and Medicine Water. He grew up hearing stories about his family and people, and has spent the past 20 years collecting Cheyenne oral accounts. This story would not be possible without him.
2. Sipe Jr. interview.
3. Grinnell, George Bird, *The Fighting Cheyennes*, (Norman, Oklahoma: University of Oklahoma Press: 1955), 170.
4. *Rocky Mountain News*, December 17, 1864.
5. Sipe Jr., interview.
6. Clyde A. Milner II, Carol A. O'Connor, Martha A. Sandweiss, eds., *The Oxford History of the American West*, (New York: Oxford University Press, 1994), 179.
7. Hoig, Stan, *The Sand Creek Massacre*, (Norman, Oklahoma: University of Oklahoma Press, 1961), 188.
8. The Bunch of Timber River was also known to the Cheyenne as the Grove of Timber Creek.
9. Sipe Jr., interview.
10. Ibid.
11. Grinnell, *The Fighting Cheyennes*, 183-193.
12. Sipe Jr., interview.

13. Hoig, Stan, *The Battle of the Washita*, (Lincoln: University of Nebraska, 1979), 128.
14. Sipe Jr., interview.
15. Ibid.
16. Day, Leon, "What Long Shot At Adobe Walls?" *True West* (March 1992): 40-43.
17. Numbers vary on the Indian dead. In a WPA interview, old-timer Henry Stroud recalled, "The slaughter was terrific and the Comanches were bewildered when they found out they were not invulnerable from to gun fire." Peter T. Leneman says in a 1937 WPA interview, as a child he was told by a Cheyenne called Old Chief Stone "that two of his sons were killed in the battle." Lineman was born July 15, 1876 at Fort Dodge, Kansas. His father worked as a freighter for the government, and thus grew up around the forts of the plains.
18. Carriker, Robert C., *Fort Supply Indian Territory: Frontier Outpost On The Plains*, (Norman, Oklahoma, University of Oklahoma Press, 1990), 89.
19. Sipe Jr., interview.
20. Ibid.
21. Sipe Jr., interview; Randolph Peters, *People of the Sacred Mountain: Close of the Staked Plains Wars*, vol. II, 898.
22. Meredith, Grace E., ed. *Girl Captives of the Cheyennes: A True Story of the Capture and Rescue of Four Pioneer Girls 1874*, (Los Angeles: Gem Publishing Company, 1927), 17-19.
23. Grinnell, *The Fighting Cheyenne*, 336.
24. Sipe Jr., interview.

Merciless Frontier

1. From the unpublished manuscript "Life Story of Queton or Esteban" by Parker McKenzie, Queton's grandson. Also from McKenzie interview with author, Mountain View, Oklahoma, Nov. 13, 1998. McKenzie died March 5, 1999 at the age of 100. McKenzie was born Nov. 15, 1897 just north of Oklahoma's Rainy Mountain in a canvas tepee.
2. McKenzie. "Life Story of Queton or Esteban;" McKenzie to author, 1998.

3. Report of Capt. Earl Van Dorn to War Department, 5 October 1858 in *Annual Report to Secretary of War, 1858-1859*, 272-274.

4. George F. Price. *Across The Continent with the Fifth Cavalry* (New York: Antiquarian Press LTD., 1959), 70.

5. W. S. Nye. *Carbine and Lance: The Story of Old Fort Sill* (Norman: University of Oklahoma Press, 1937), 25.

6. Maj. Gen. David Twiggs to Army Headquarters, 6 July, 1858, in *Annual Report to Secretary of War, 1858-1859*, 258-259.

7. Nye. *Carbine and Lance*, 23-24.

8. *United States, Complainant, v. State of Texas,* Supreme Court of the United States, October term, 1894 (Washington: Judd and Detweiler, 1894), 683-685. Case features eyewitness testimony from U.S. Army veterans of the campaign.

9. Nye. *Carbine and Lance*, 24-25.

10. Van Dorn to War Department, 5 October 1858 in *Annual Report to Secretary of War, 1858-1859*, 272-274.

11. Nye. *Carbine and Lance*, 25-26.

12. Van Dorn to War Department, 5 October 1858 in *Annual Report to Secretary of War, 1858-1859*, 272.

13. Ibid., 273.

14. Nye. *Carbine and Lance*, 25.

15. McKenzie to author, 1998.

16. Nye. *Carbine and Lance*, 28; Price. *Across The Continent with the Fifth Cavalry*, 70-71.

17. Van Dorn to War Department, 5 October 1858 in *Annual Report to Secretary of War, 1858-1859*, 272-274; Nye. *Carbine and Lance*, 29.

18. Ibid., 273.

19. William E. Burnett. "Lieutenant Wm. E. Burnett: Notes on Removal of Indiand from Texas to Indian Territory." Edited by Raymond Estep. *The Chronicles of Oklahoma*, XXXVIII, 283-284.

20. Ibid., 283.

21. Van Dorn to War Department, 5 October 1858 in *Annual Report to Secretary of War, 1858-1859*, 273.

22. Report of Capt. Earl Van Dorn to War Department, 11 October 1858 in *Annual Report to Secretary of War, 1858-1859*, 275.

23. McKenzie to author, 1998; Nye. *Carbine and Lance*, 123; Paula Mitchell Marks "The Legend of Britt Johnson." *True West* (March 1986), 26-30.

Buffalo Wallow Fight
1. *The Oklahoman*, 14 April, 1929.
2. Ibid.
3. Handbook of Texas Online, Second Battle Of Adobe Walls, http://www.tsha.utexas.edu/handbook/online/articles/aa/btal.html (accessed November 12, 2006)
4. Olive K. Dixon. *Life of "Billy" Dixon: Plainsman, Scout and Pioneer* (Dallas: The Southern Press, 1914), 199.
5. Dixon, *Life of "Billy" Dixon*, 200.
6. Ibid.
7. Ibid., 201.
8. Ibid.; Joe F. Taylor, ed., "The Indian Campaign on the Staked Plains, 1874-1875: Military Correspondence from War Department Adjutant General's Office, File 2815-1874. *Panhandle-Plains Historical Review* (v. 34, 1961), 51.
9. Dixon, *Life of "Billy" Dixon*, 202.
10. John L. McCarty. *Adobe Walls Bride: The Story of Billy and Olive King Dixon* (San Antonio: The Naylor Company, 1955), 63.
11. Ibid.
12. Ibid.
13. Ibid., 64.
14. Ibid., 66.
15. Dixon, *Life of "Billy" Dixon*, 207.
16. Ibid., 209.
17. Ibid., 211.
18. Ibid., 213.
19. Ibid., 214.
20. Nelson A. Miles. *Personal Recollections And Observations of General Nelson A. Miles* (Chicago/New York: The Werner Company, 1896), 173-174; *The Oklahoman*, 14 April, 1929.
21. Handbook of Texas Online, Amos Chapman, http://www.tsha.utexas.edu/handbook/online/articles/aa/btal.html (accessed November 12, 2006)

22. Handbook of Texas Online, William Dixon, http://www.tsha.utexas.edu/handbook/online/articles/aa/btal.html (accessed November 12, 2006)

23. Handbook of Texas Online, Amos Chapman; *The Oklahoman*, 14 April, 1929.

24. Dixon, *Life of "Billy" Dixon*, 214.

Ron J. Jackson, Jr. is an award-winning reporter and author whose career spans 22 years. He is the author of *Alamo Legacy: Alamo Descendants Remember The Alamo* (Eakin Press, 1997), *Chiseled In Stone: The Saga of Rocky, Oklahoma Territory* (Nortex Press, 2000), and numerous magazine articles on the western frontier. He is presently a staff writer for *The Oklahoman* newspaper in Oklahoma City, and lives on Oklahoma's western prairie with his wife, Jeannia, and their four children—Joseph, Ashley, Tristan, and Missouri.

www.ingramcontent.com/pod-product-compliance
Lightning Source LLC
LaVergne TN
LVHW051525070426
835507LV00023B/3302